Portrait of a Suburbanite

Portrait of a Suburbanite

POEMS OF CHOI SEUNG-JA

Translated by
Kim Eunju

East Asia Program
Cornell University
Ithaca, New York 14853

The Cornell East Asia Series is published by the Cornell University East Asia Program (distinct from Cornell University Press). We publish books on a variety of scholarly topics relating to East Asia as a service to the academic community and the general public. Address submission inquiries to CEAS Editorial Board, East Asia Program, Cornell University, 140 Uris Hall, Ithaca, New York 14853-7601.

This publication is supported by a grant from the Korea Literature Translation Institute.

Cover Image: Li Shiyi
Number 173 in the Cornell East Asia Series
Copyright © 2015 Cornell East Asia Program. All rights reserved.
ISSN: 1050-2955
ISBN: 978-1-939161-53-6 hardcover
ISBN: 978-1-939161-73-4 paperback
ISBN: 978-1-942242-73-4 e-book
Library of Congress Control Number: 2015939305

▫▫◾ CONTENTS ◾▫▫

BIOGRAPHICAL CHRONOLOGY

1952   Born in Yeon-gi, Southern Chungcheong Province, South Korea

1971   Graduated Sudo Girl's High School

1971   Studied German Literature in Korea University, Seoul

1979   Debuted in the journal, *Literature and Intellect*

1981   Published a first volume of poetry, *Love of This Age*

1984   Published a second volume of poetry, *Merry Diary*

1989   Published a poetry selection, *Would You Teach Me a Bird*

1991   Published a third volume of poetry, *House of Memory*

1991   Published a poetry selection, *Portrait of a Suburbanite*

1993   Published a fourth volume of poetry, *My Tomb, Green*

1993   Participated in the Iowa International Writing Program

1998   Published a fifth volume of poetry, *Lovers*

2010   Published a sixth volume of poetry, *Distant Because Lonely*

2010   Received the Mount Jiri Award

2010   Received the Daesan Foundation Award

2011   Published a seventh volume of poetry, *Written on Water*

☐☐☐ INTRODUCTION ☐☐☐

This volume is a translation of Choi Seung-ja's 1991 anthology titled *Portrait of a Suburbanite*. Published in the series "100 Prominent Korean Poets" by *Mirae* Press, the poems that appear in this volume were selected from four of Choi's previous works, *Love of This Age* (1981), *Merry Diary* (1984), *House of Memory* (1991), and *My Tomb, Green* (1993).

Since some poems were composed as early as 1973, this selection begins near the midpoint of President Park Chung-hee's eighteen years of military rule and ends in 1991, near the dawn of a democratic South Korea. It is this era of oppression and popular resistance that became a monumental turning point in Korean literary history, especially in poetry. While the output of novels slowed because of unprecedentedly harsh censorship, Korean poets in the eighties overcame fear and self-censorship to produce many influential works, which led many Koreans to regard the eighties as the Age of Poetry.

One of the most decisive events defining this literary era was the publication of Choi Seung-ja's debut volume, *Love of This Age*, in 1981. Breaking down ossified aesthetics and conventions in existing Korean poetry, Choi experimented with the fixed form and persona of lyric poetry. She modernized the traditional language and attitude of love poems; suggested a model of the new women, who are unsilenced, carnal, and political; and imbued the intense sociopolitical poems with tender lyricism.

Despite Choi's prominence as a modern poet, English translations of her poems have only been published in a few anthologies. The present volume represents the first substantial English introduction to Choi's poetry as well as serves as an invaluable literary record of the eighties, in which the most fundamental social transformation occurred in modern Korean history.

viii

Portrait of a Suburbanite

THE POET'S BACKGROUND

Choi Seung-ja was born in 1952 in the midst of the Korean War (1950–1953). When she was ten years old her family moved to Seoul from the tiny village of Yeon-gi, South Chungcheong Province. In Seoul she witnessed the full span of the "miracle on the Han River, South Korea's dramatic economic growth between 1961 and 1996, which made the country into a role model for many developing countries in Asia.[1] Choi attended Sudo Girls' High School and in 1971 entered Korea University to study German Literature but her studies kept getting interrupted by South Korea's turbulent politics.

Throughout the decades of postwar reconstruction, Korea's military rulers continually thwarted the democratic aspirations of their citizens. As it happens, Korea University had been a hotbed of student dissent ever since campus protests ignited the "April 19 Revolution" in 1960.[2] In response, the military regime often shut down the university and expelled politically engaged students at the slightest provocation. Although (or because) Choi was the first female student editor of Korea University's literary magazine, this fate eventually also befell her. Since a writer's success often

---

[1] Miracle on the Han River: This phrase originally comes from the "miracle on the Rhine," which was used to describe the economic rebirth of then West Germany after World War II. When General Park Chung-hee seized power in 1961, South Korea had an annual per capita income of less than $80, but in 2013, according to the List of Cities by GDP, the country had transformed to the world's fourth largest metropolitan economy (http://en.wikipedia.org/wiki/List_of_cities_by_GDP, accessed March 31, 2015).

[2] April 19 Revolution was a popular uprising and a democratization movement led by labor and student groups against a nationwide election fraud in 1960. The events were touched off by the discovery in Masan Harbor of the body of a student killed by a tear-gas shell in demonstrations against vote-rigging in the March 15 elections. Koreans had been under Syngman Rhee's long-term seizure of power for twelve years (1948–1960) and were ready to stand up against his dictatorship. South Koreans accused Rhee of holding corrupt elections and made him resign, thus overthrowing the autocratic First Republic of South Korea and making a transition to the Second Republic.

hinges upon the assistance of mentors and patrons, this expulsion could have been the end of Choi's career, but Choi was undaunted by such adversity. After leaving the university she worked for a small publishing company as a copy editor and began a career as a translator. In 1979 she made her literary debut with five poems appearing in the prominent journal, *Literature and Intellect,* including the renowned poem "Love of This Age." Her first complete volume, *Love of This Age,* in 1981 immediately became a bestseller. From 1984 to 1993 she published three more volumes of poetry and several works of translation. In 1993 she participated in the Iowa International Writing Program and in 1998 published *Lovers,* another volume of poetry.

The turn of the millennium began a difficult period for Choi. One interview conducted in 2010 revealed an emaciated Choi who, weighing barely seventy-five pounds at just under five feet tall, spoke frankly about her diagnosis of schizophrenia in 1991. On top of the debilitating symptoms of the illness, Choi had been suffering extreme poverty, isolation, and homelessness. In 2008, no longer able to sleep or eat, Choi entered a mental hospital in Pohang. Yet in 2010, after years of silence, Choi reemerged from the hospital with her sixth volume, *Distant Because Lonely.* Within a year this work sold over a million copies and became another bestseller.

Thirty-one years after her literary debut, Choi received long-delayed recognition from two major camps in the Korean literary establishment. In 2010 she received the Mount Jiri Award from the progressive-realist camp followed by the Daesan Foundation Award from her own lyrical-modernist camp. Defining her works as the fatal and turbulent viral factor that affected an age, judges of the Mount Jiri Award announced Choi's authenticity as the reason for their choice. Recognizing the lasting significance of Choi's works in the political struggle for democratic reform, poet Shin Kyong-rim, head judge of the competition, lamented that "offering this Mount Jiri award should have happened a long time ago. The literary world has been too inconsiderate." In 2011, Choi published her latest volume, *Written on Water.*

RECEPTION OF THE POET'S STYLE

With her iconoclastic style and wide tonal range, Choi made a striking impression on the Korean literary world. However, despite her popularity and influence, Choi had a difficult time gaining widespread critical recognition. While the political situation certainly was a factor, critics in the early eighties had difficulty placing Choi's work in the proper interpretive context. It was not until the development of feminist and poststructural theory in Korea in the late eighties and early nineties that a critical readership developed that had the resources to recognize the range and scope of Choi's poetic innovations. Before this, the first wave of critical reception still placed Choi's poetry in the generic context of traditional lyrical themes and personae regardless of the fact that Choi aimed to rattle and dismantle them. In addition, Korean women have had a long experience with a modernizing Korea that traditional literary forms could not address. With haunting lyrical power coupled with an experimental avant-garde spirit, Choi brought to Korean poetry a challenging and honest account of women's contemporary experiences. In doing so, Choi often defied her readers' expectations, many of which were shaped by the traditional lyric and its image of the virtuous Korean woman. Earlier twentieth-century Korean poets had modernized many oral poetic devices to develop an open-form, free-verse vehicle to contrast with the rigid patterns and rules of the traditional lyric. Nonetheless, the subtlest and most persistent premise of the lyric persona largely remained in effect.

The persona of the lyricist is a second-order projection, a portrait of the poet as a speaking individual that the reader constructs from the particulars of the poem. The emphasis on the lyric persona's propriety and decorum continued into the modern age. In the case of women especially, the traditional lyric often showcased a persona with elegantly expressed, well-adjusted emotions. Even when women's lyrical personae suffer from love, they still express proper sentiments in carefully crafted poems full of respectful resignation mixed with hopeful loyalty. Not only had the lyrical persona become a poetic constraint, but the long association between lyrical elegance and emotional regulation had turned lyric poetry into a psychological corral, especially for women poets. This lingering persistence of the lyric form and persona contributed to Choi's decades-long critical marginalization. The traditional Korean lyric was widely regarded as a medium of edification. Each poem would stage the achievement of the lyric persona, and if negative emotions appeared at all, it was only so the persona could demonstrate how to sublimate and transcend them. Choi's poems, however, repeatedly betray these expectations and transgress the limits of self-censorship. Much of the beauty of Choi's poetry comes from acknowledging each emotion, however dark or threatening, and lingering over its contours and illustrating its logic. In this way, Choi's poems mark a radical departure from traditional lyrics filled with edifying ideas and tranquilizing sighs.

Yet the predominance of the Korean lyric often led critics to treat the emotional dynamics in Choi's poetry as simply inappropriate. Even as they recognized the unprecedented achievement of her poetry, rather than analyzing the aesthetic effect of Choi's poems, many of her critics focused on the psychological status of the poet. But collapsing poet and persona transforms each poem into the poet's self-confession. From this perspective, a poet who presents an extreme or improper lyrical persona raises the suspicion of pathology, which led to the ironic situation of a popular and widely read poet who was dismissed or diminished by many in the literary establishment. At first, many realist critics regarded emerging deconstructionists including Choi as "escapists" or "word-players," and some established lyricist critics blamed deconstructionist poetry for ruining traditional lyricism. Even after many years of popular support and the serious evaluation of young critics, it was only the male deconstructionists who were seizing the literary awards. The literary authorities denied recognition of Choi Seung-ja despite her undeniable popularity and accomplishment. Yet the same critics quickly embraced other women whose poetry exhibited the decorum and charm typical of the traditional lyrical persona. However, even as Choi was repeatedly snubbed, Korean poetry itself was undergoing irrevocable change. Choi pioneered to break many topics of taboo in women's poetry such as those of body, sexuality, and diction, and this delayed recognition was indeed the price she paid as her poetry transgressed those taboos and broke out of the orbit of traditional literary expectations.

THE POETIC EVOCATION OF
KOREAN DEMOGRAPHY

The title of this volume, *Portrait of a Suburbanite (Jubyonin-ui Chosang)*, provides a key to understanding Choi's poetics and the time in which she wrote. Though one might translate *Jubyonin* as "the marginalized" or "the alienated" or "the peripheral," the term "suburbanite" was chosen for several reasons.

First, a close look at the poem from which the volume's title derives reveals that the modern city is the specific setting, which the other generic terms failed to suggest. Unlike in some Western cases, in Korea there has been no such voluntary exodus from its capital city toward suburbia. The Korean suburbanite's attention remains fixed on Seoul, its capital and the foremost economic, political, cultural, and also residential center of South Korea. To access better education and greater opportunity, Koreans constantly move toward Seoul, which leads to the ongoing growth of the city and its suburbs. With a population of over ten million, almost a quarter of South Korea's population, Seoul is the largest city proper in the OECD.[3] By 2007, Seoul, together with its suburbs, known as *Sudogwon*, had become the world's second largest metropolitan area with over 25.6 million inhabitants, almost half of South Korea's population. In 2014, it is estimated that an average of 1.2 million people commute daily between Seoul and its surrounding suburbs such as Gyeonggi-do and Incheon.[4]

Second, as spatial metaphor, the suburbanite carries overtones of a socioeconomic, political, and even existential condition that Choi depicts as common to the majority of Koreans in her time. In

---

[3] The Organisation for Economic Co-operation and Development (OECD) is an international economic organization comprising thirty-four countries founded in 1961 to stimulate economic progress and world trade.

[4] Statistics Korea, November 18 2014, Analysis of the Main Characteristics of the Life Cycle. Mail Kyongje & mk.co.kr, http://news.mk.co.kr.

South Korean context the term "suburbanite" depicts the keen sense of alienation and ennui as well as references to specific geographical and psychological connotations that make the title historically and demographically relevant. Choi's suburbanites suffer from the sense that a better life exists elsewhere, that the suburban life is a pale shadow of the urban one.

Choi does not feature suburbanites existing "in their place" as if living within their natural environment. Instead, she depicts the feeling of anxiety suburbanites have concerning their unnatural placelessness. Choi vividly presents the suburbanite as being in a state of fluctuation and frustration, as simultaneously ambitious and complacent, aspiring and resigned, engaged and disaffected. By mapping social hierarchy onto the landscape, Choi portrays the political, economic, and existential displacement of the suburbanite.

Third and finally, the figure of the "suburbanite" unifies what might appear to be distinct and unrelated moments in these poems. Since the plight of the politically and economically marginalized suburbanite was a commonplace condition of the age, Choi depicts alienation in a way that addresses not only the abject underclass— as many contemporary progressive realists had done—but the alienated multitude of Koreans as well. Indeed, Koreans living in this era's brew of an age-old Confucian patriarchy have adapted to military rule and market domination. Choi's "suburbanite" is thus more inclusive in its sense of the excluded: instead of referring to a delimited group, it describes the most common condition. With the "suburbanite" referring to a demographic that includes the poet herself, Choi employs this ambiguity to pivot between subjective and objective perspectives. As she evoked her contemporaries' mute longing and undocumented suffering, with the figure of the suburbanite she succeeded in redrawing connections between Koreans at a time of great social fragmentation.

DECONSTRUCTION AND FEMINISM

After the assassination of President Park Chung-hee in 1979, the eighties began with his successor, Chun Du-hwan, perpetrating yet another coup d'état, provoking nationwide protests that culminated with the Gwangju massacre of many prodemocracy demonstrators. It was in this crucible of political repression and social fragmentation that Korea's era of poetry was born. Alongside the leading poets committed to progressive change through social realism, another group of young modernists emerged from the lyricist tradition armed with many of their distinctive poetic techniques critics later described as a common "deconstructive" approach to poetry. Members of this group included Choi Seung-ja, Hwang Ji-u,[5] Yi Sŏng-bok, [6] and Park Nam-cheol.[7]

---

[5] Hwang Ji-u (1952–) studied aesthetics at Seoul National University, philosophy at Sogang University, and currently is a professor in the Department of Creative Writing, Hansin University. He began his literary career in 1980 by winning the spring literary contest organized by the Chungang Ilbo with his poem "Yonhyok" (Chronology). By implementing various experimental techniques such as collage, parody, visual letter composite, montage, documentary, he deconstructed the fixed form of lyric poetry, demystified its ideology, and thus exposed the fragmented reality and oppressive politics of the time. His published volumes of poetry include *Even the Birds Are Leaving the World* (1983), *Gyeoul namurobuteo bom namu ero* (From the winter trees to the spring trees, 1985), *Na neun neo da* (I am you, 1987).

[6] Yi Sŏng-bok (1952–) earned both his MA and BA from Seoul National University and has taught French literature at Keimyung University in Daegu. He made his debut in 1977 by publishing his poem "Jeong-deun You-gwak" (My endeared brothel) in the quarterly literary magazine *Literature and Intelligence*. In his first volume, *When Will the Rolling Stone Awaken* (1980), he shockingly magnified 1980's corruption and violence through the glass of a family life. He did not reconstruct the reality with language but exposed reality by distorting the language itself. For this avant-garde experiment he implemented a variety of poetic devices such as clashing incongruous poetic words, stuttering, sentence dismantling, and imagery repetition. His published volumes of poetry include *When Does the Rolling Stone Awaken* (1980), *South Sea, Silk Mountain* (1986), and *End of That Summer* (1990). In 2010, translation of his poetry selection *I Heard Life Calling Me: Poems of Yi Sŏng-bok* was published in English by Cornell University East Asia Series.

[7] Park Nam-cheol (1953–2014) earned both his MA and BA in Korean language and literature from Kyung Hee University. He made his debut in 1979 by publishing three of his poems, including "Yeon Naligi" (Flying a kite), in the quarterly literary magazine *Literature and Intelligence*. From the mid 1980s, he became known as a leading deconstructionist. His poetry is famous for its dismantled form, infiltrated anger, and satire. Some critics consider him the most extreme deconstructionist of all for his concern was purely focused on the language itself rather than the reality or the self. His published volumes of poetry include *Yet I Will Live* (1982), *Men on Earth* (1984), *Anti-chronological Investigation* (1988).

Since the sixties and the collapse of any pretense of democratic rule, Korean poets had begun to attack the idol of the father as a stand-in for the patriarchal face of the military regime, but poets of the eighties knew that the father rules as more than an image. "Forbidden to speak, I destroy the form," famously wrote poet Hwang Ji-u.[8] In this era the iconoclasm of the father image evolved into the deconstruction of the father's language, that is, iconoclasm developed into logoclasm.

Speaking with a fierce sense of equality and independence, Choi's poetry battled ossified forms of language not only on the political but also the personal front. Like her male colleagues, Choi parodied and critiqued the idol of the father, but even further, she insightfully explored irreverent content to reveal the gendered constraints of the lyric form. In particular, Choi exposed the idolatrous power of the lover, the basis of exploitation and injustice at the most intimate level. On top of their political disempowerment as citizens, the private and domestic alienation of women as daughters, lovers, and wives forms a deep stratum of repression. When Choi's women personae broke this long silence of compliance nurtured by the traditional lyric and voiced themselves as exploited and traumatized, yet fearless and tenacious human beings, the shock of this transgression shook the nation. In turn it demonstrated how long and how powerfully the gender constrictions had been imposed on Korean women.

At last Choi's critical eye even turns upon itself, when the next stage of her iconoclasm scrutinizes the idols of womanhood. Whether addressing maidenhood or matronage, daughter or mother, Choi's poems idolize no variant of woman. Rather, Choi places womanhood in a context of universal transformations, great cyclical processes with such cosmic significance that they are ultimately depersonalizing. In addition, Choi's portrait of the alienated woman exposes the fault lines of Korean women's

---

[8] "Fundamentally, literature is the fruit harvested from not only the desire to express what one wants to, but also the ambition and challenge to express what one can't or is forbidden to. Then, how to convert what's impossible to what is possible? How to climb up the ladder to silence? Forbidden to speak, I destroy the form. Or rather, I conventionalize the destruction." Hwang Ji-u, *The Signal between People*, (Seoul: Ganmadang, 1986) pp. 100–101.

traditional acculturation. In this way Choi strips away the nostalgic idealization of the family, the romantic glamorization of love, and the therapeutic normalization of modern life. By doing so she creates a new kind of lyric poetry never before seen in Korea, a tightrope walk between explosively intimate details coupled with an encoded social critique.

With these deep links between women's perspectives and poetic form, Choi's deconstruction of women's roles would make her a natural ally of feminism. Indeed, when Korean feminist theory emerged in the late eighties, it embraced Choi from the start. Choi herself, however, has both embraced and downplayed the connection between her poetry and feminism. For example, she once revealed her expansive interpretation of feminism by saying, "Whatever the -ism is, for [a work] to gain power not simply as a social movement but as literature itself, it must be based on individualism and humanism, and at the same time it must sublimate itself to those dimensions. If feminism wants to exercise its power in literature rather than in a movement, it might have to give more interest to all things individualistic, existential, and humanistic rather than feminism itself. Otherwise it is possible for feminism to become a simplistic womanism."[9]

CONCLUSION

With explosive language coupled with bold and sometimes grotesque imagery, Choi Seung-ja established a distinctive poetic idiom that ranged far beyond the limited emotional scope typical of much Korean poetry. Choi's deconstructive poetry both reflects its age and constitutes an essential artifact for understanding the alienation endemic to Korean life under military rule and accelerating modernization. In an era of censorship, when free speech survived only in coded form, Choi expanded the scope of Korean poetry to depict the political despair and violence of the age, a task that Korean lyricists usually left to their progressive-realist counterparts. In doing so Choi evoked a humanism that

[9] Choi Seung-ja, *Eotteon Namudeureun* (Some Trees) (Seoul: Segyesa, 1995), p. 159.

includes but surpasses feminism. Clearly, this humanism is far from traditional. Her poems do not set out to present an authentic self, describe the individual's legitimate roles, or establish women's proper place. Instead, her poems address placelessness as the common experience during the Age of Poetry. It is on this common ground between all suburbanites where the poet writes so that another, better, humanism might one day be born. Choi Seung-ja's work thus stands as a monument to artistic courage in a dangerous and volatile era in Korean history.

Kim Eunju
(in collaboration with
Christopher Roberts)

■■■ I ■■■

이 시대의 사랑

LOVE OF THIS AGE

일찍이 나는

일찍이 나는 아무것도 아니었다.
마른 빵에 핀 곰팡이
벽에다 누고 또 눈 지린 오줌 자국
아직도 구더기에 뒤덮인 천 년 전에 죽은 시체.

아무 부모도 나를 키워주지 않았다.
쥐구멍에서 잠들고 벼룩의 간을 내먹고
아무 데서나 하염없이 죽어가면서
일찍이 나는 아무 것도 아니었다.

떨어지는 유성처럼 우리가
잠시 스쳐갈 때 그러므로,
나를 안다고 말하지 말라.
나는너를모른다 나는너를모른다.
너당신그대, 행복
너, 당신, 그대, 사랑

내가 살아 있다는 것,
그것은 영원한 루머에 지나지 않는다.

이 시대의 사랑

BEFORE, I WAS

Before, I was nothing.
A mold on dry bread
a foul stain repeatedly pissed onto a wall
a thousand-year-old corpse still covered with maggots.

No parent fostered me.
Sleeping in rat holes, feeding on flea livers,
dying endlessly anywhere,
before, I was nothing.

When we flash past each other
like falling stars, therefore,
don't say you know me.
Idon'tknowyou Idon'tknowyou.
Youdeardarling, Happiness
You, Dear, Darling, Love

That I'm alive,
it's merely a perpetual rumor.

□□□ | □□□

개 같은 가을이

개 같은 가을이 쳐들어온다.
매독 같은 가을.
그리고 죽음은, 황혼 그 마비된
한쪽 다리에 찾아온다.

모든 사물이 습기를 잃고
모든 길들의 경계선이 문드러진다.
레코드에 담긴 옛 가수의 목소리가 시들고
여보세요 죽선이 아니니 죽선이지 죽선아
전화선이 허공에서 수신인을 잃고
한번 떠나간 애인들은 꿈에도 다시 돌아오지 않는다.

그리고 그리고 괴어 있는 기억의 廢水가
한없이 말 오줌 냄새를 풍기는 세월의 봉놋방에서
나는 부시시 죽었다 깨어난 목소리로 묻는다.
어디 만큼 왔나 어디까지 가야
강물은 바다가 될 수 있을까.

4   이 시대의 사랑

DOG-LIKE AUTUMN

A dog-like autumn invades.
A syphilitic autumn.
And death, descends upon the dusk
upon that paralytic leg.

All things lose their moisture,
all roads crumble at the curbs.
An old singer's voice withers on a phonograph,
Hello Is this Juk-suhn Isn't this Juk-suhn Hey Juk-suhn
phone-lines lose their receivers in the empty air,
and once departed, lovers never return even in dreams.

And and in time's tavern where the stagnant wastewater
of memory infinitely emits a horse-urine stench
I ask in the deadened voice of the just-resurrected.
How far have I come, how far have I to go
till a river becomes the sea.

혹은 살의랄까 자폭

한밤중 흐릿한 불빛 속에
책상 위에 놓인 송곳이
내 두개골의 殺意처럼 빛난다.
고독한 이빨을 갈고 있는 살의,
아니 그것은 사랑.

칼날이 허공에서 빛난다.
내 모가지를 향해 내려오는
그러나 순간순간 영원히 멈춰 있는.

쳐라 쳐라 내 목을 쳐라.
내 모가지가 땅바닥에 덩그렁
떨어지는 소리를, 땅바닥에 떨어진
내 모가지의 귀로 듣고 싶고
그리고서야 땅바닥에 떨어진
나의 눈은 눈감을 것이다.

LOVE OR MURDEROUS INTENT
OR SELF-DESTRUCTION

At midnight in dim light
an awl on a desk
shines like the murderous intent in my skull.
A murderous intent grinding its lonely teeth,
no, it is love.

A blade shines in the empty air.
Descending towards my neck
yet moment by moment forever still.

Cut Cut Cut off my head.
I want to hear the sound of my head
falling thump on the ground
with the ears of my own fallen head
and only then on the ground
will my eyes close themselves.

해남 대흥사에서

깊은 밤 강물은 바다로 흘러들고
우리의 손은 사랑하는 사람의 손을 찾는다.
우리 몸 속에서 오래 잠자던 물살이
문득 깨어나 흐르고

비가 오리라
바다 건너서
그대의 땅을 적시며.

산사의 계곡
하늘의 빈 술잔엔
서푸른 취기의 바람이 일렁이고
지금 어느 산맥 뒤에서
두 연인의 손이 만난다.

■■■ | ■■·

AT DAEHEUNG TEMPLE[1] IN HAENAM

In deep night a river finds the sea
and our hands seek beloved hands.
The long-sleeping current in our body
suddenly wakes and flows

and rain will come
crossing the sea
drenching your land.

In the valley of the mountain temple
in the empty glass of the sky
the ferocious drunken wind billows
and now behind a mountain range
the hands of two lovers converge.[2]

---

[1] The Daeheung Temple in Haenam (called Daeheungsa or Daedunsa) is a prominent temple of the Jogye Order of Korean Buddhism. Though its exact date of construction is uncertain, many historians hold that it was built during the Shilla dynasty either in 426 by the monk Jeong-gwan or in 544 by Ahdo-hwasang.

[2] In the original publication this poem included the dedication, "To the mom and dad of Eun-jee, hoping that they will read this poem as Eun-jee's conception dream" (*Love of This Age*, p. 16).,

네게로

흐르는 물처럼
네게로 가리.
물에 풀리는 알콜처럼
알콜에 엉기는 니코틴처럼
니코틴에 달라붙는 카페인처럼
네게로 가리.
혈관을 타고 흐르는 매독균처럼
삶을 거머잡는 죽음처럼.

이 시대의 사랑

TO YOU

Like running water
I'll come to you.
Like alcohol diffusing in water
like nicotine clotting in alcohol
like caffeine clinging to nicotine
I'll come to you.
Like syphilis riding through veins
like death seizing life.

여자들과 사내들

사랑은 언제나
벼락처럼 왔다가
정전처럼 끊겨지고
갑작스런 배고픔으로
찾아오는 이별.

사내의 눈물 한 방울
망막의 막막대해로 삼켜지고
돌아서면 그뿐
사내들은 물결처럼 흘러가지만,

허연 외로움의 뇌수 흘리며
잊으려고 잊으려고 여자들은
바람을 향해 돌아서지만,

땅거미 질 무렵
길고긴 울음 끝에
공복의 술 몇 잔,
불현듯 낄낄거리며 떠오르는 사랑,
그리움의 아수라장.

(계속)

이 시대의 사랑

WOMEN AND MEN

Love always
comes on like lightning
cuts off like a blackout
then the farewell
befalling like sudden hunger.

Diffusing one tear-drop
into the retina's vast sea,
once turned away then that's all
though men flow wave-like away.

Spilling white loneliness from the brain
to forget, to forget
though women turn around to face the wind.

At dusk
at the end of a long weep
a few drinks on empty stomachs,
suddenly surfacing giggling love,
Asuras' battlefield of yearning.[3]

(continued)

---

[3] Asura-jang, translated here as "Asuras' battlefield," developed from the Buddhist notion of Asuras, which refers to a species of "demigods" or antagonistic spirits broadly derived from the wicked Asuras of Hinduism. Classical Hinduism, particularly in the 16th section of the Baghavad Gita in the Indian epic, *Mahabharata,* developed the psychological sense of the Asuras as the warring appetites and emotions. Many passages liken the play of these malignant psychological forces to the battlefield where the epic war takes place.

(여자들과 사내들)

흐르는 별 아래
이 도회의 더러운 지붕 위에서,
여자들과 사내들은
서로의 무덤을 베고 누워
내일이면 후줄근해질 과거를
열심히 빨아 널고 있습니다.

이 시대의 사랑

□□■ | ■□□

(Women and Men)

Under the flowing stars
upon this city's dirty roofs,
women and men
pillow their heads on each other's tombs
and earnestly launder the pasts
that will just get dingy tomorrow.[4]

---

[4] In the original publication, this poem was dedicated "to Kim Jeong-suk" (*Love of This Age*, p. 18).

삼십 세

이렇게 살 수도 없고 이렇게 죽을 수도 없을 때
서른 살은 온다.
시큰거리는 치통 같은 흰 손수건을 내저으며
놀라 부릅뜬 흰자위로 애원하며.

내 꿈은 말이야, 위장에서 암세포가 싹트고
장가가는 거야, 간장에서 독이 반짝 눈뜬다.
두 눈구멍에 죽음의 붉은 신호등이 켜지고
피는 젤리 손톱은 톱밥 머리칼은 철사
끝없는 광물질의 안개를 뚫고
몸뚱어리 없는 그림자가 나아가고
이제 새로 꿀 꿈이 없는 새들은
추억의 골고다로 날아가 뼈를 묻고
흰 손수건이 떨어뜨려지고
부릅뜬 흰자위가 감긴다.

오 행복행복행복한 항복
기쁘다우리 철판깔았네

AGE THIRTY

When one can neither live like this nor die like this
thirty comes.
Waving a white handkerchief like a throbbing toothache
pleading with shocked white eyes wide open.

Let me tell you my dream, in the stomach a cancer cell
    sprouts,
It's taking a wife, in the liver poison pops open its eyes.
In the eye sockets red lights flash death,
Blood is jelly Fingernail is sawdust Hair is wire
through that endless fog of mineral matter
a shadow without body breaks,
birds with no new dreams to dream now
fly to memory's Golgotha and bury their bones,
a white handkerchief is dropped,
the wide white eyes are shut.

Oh happyhappyhappy surrender
Delightedweare brazenandbrassy[5]

---

[5] Korean "(eolgure) cheol-pan ggaranne" means "having covered (one's face) with a sheet of steel." It is a common expression for being thick skinned, shameless, or pushy.

비 오는 날의 재회

하늘과 방 사이로
빗줄기는 슬픔의 악보를 옮긴다
외로이 울고 있는 커피잔
無爲를 마시고 있는 꽃 두 송이
누가 내 머릿속에서 오래 멈춰 있던
현을 고르고 있다.

가만히 비집고 들어갈 수 있을까.
흙 위에 괴는 빗물처럼
다시 네 속으로 스며들 수 있을까.
투명한 유리벽 너머로
너는 생생히 웃는데
지나간 시간을 나는 증명할 수 없다
네 입맞춤 속에 녹아 있던 모든 것을
다시 만져볼 수 없다.

젖은 창 밖으로 비행기 한 대가 기울고 있다
이제 결코 닿을 수 없는 시간 속으로

이 시대의 사랑

RAINY DAY REUNION

Between the sky and the room
rain-stems transcribe scores of sadness.
One coffee cup weeping forlorn
two flowers drinking ennui—
someone tunes the strings
long still in my head.

Can I gently press through?
Can I seep into you again
like rainwater pooled on soil?
Though you smile vividly
beyond the clear glass wall,
I cannot attest to times past.
I cannot touch again
all that dissolved in your kiss.

Out the streaming window an airplane tilts
into the time now impossible to reach.

청파동을 기억하는가

겨울 동안 너는 다정했었다.
눈(雪)의 흰 손이 우리의 잠을 어루만지고
우리가 꽃잎처럼 포개져
따뜻한 땅속을 떠돌 동안엔

봄이 오고 너는 갔다
라일락꽃이 귀신처럼 피어나고
먼 곳에서도 너는 웃지 않았다.
자주 너의 눈빛이 셀로판지 구겨지는 소리를 냈고
너의 목소리가 쇠꼬챙이처럼 나를 찔렀고
그래, 나는 소리 없이 오래 찔렸다.

찔린 몸으로 지렁이처럼 기어서라도,
가고 싶다 네가 있는 곳으로.
너의 따뜻한 불빛 안으로 숨어들어가
다시 한번 최후로 찔리면서
한없이 오래 죽고 싶다.

그리고 지금, 주인 없는 해진 신발마냥
내가 빈 벌판을 헤맬 때
청파동을 기억하는가

우리가 꽃잎처럼 포개져
눈 덮인 꿈속을 떠돌던
몇 세기 전의 겨울을.

이 시대의 사랑

DO YOU REMEMBER CHEONGPA VILLAGE?[6]

During the winter you were sweet
while snow's white hands soothed our sleep
while we drifted warm underground
overlapped like petals.

Spring came and you were gone.
Lilacs blossomed like ghosts
and even from afar you didn't smile.
Often your eyes made crinkling cellophane sounds
and your voice pierced me like an iron skewer
and yes, I was pierced for so long silently.

Even if I have to crawl like a punctured worm,
I want to go where you are.
Creep into your warm light
and pierced again one last time
I want to die endlessly forever.

And now, like a lost tattered shoe
as I stray through an empty field,
do you remember Cheongpa Village?

That winter many centuries ago
when we drifted in snow-covered dreams
overlapped like petals.

---

[6] Choi worked at a small publishing company near Cheongpa Village, which was a historically underdeveloped area consisting of numerous unauthorized houses built around the Cheongye watercourse in Gurogu, Seoul. It is also near Pyeonghwa Market where the Workers Movement started in 1970. In 2010, the government started developing the area.

우우, 널 버리고 싶어

식은 사랑 한 짐 부려놓고
그는 세상 꿈을 폭파하기 위해
나를 잠가놓고 떠났다.
나는 도로 닫혀졌다.

비인 집에서 나는
정신이 아프고
인생이 아프다.
배고픈 저녁마다
아픈 정신은
문간에 나가앉아,
세상 꿈이 남아 있는 한
결코 돌아오지 않을 그의
발자국 소리를 기다린다.

우우, 널 버리고 싶어
이 기다림을 벗고 싶어
돈 많은 애인을 얻고 싶어
따뜻한 무덤을 마련하고 싶어

천천히 취해가는 술을 마시다
천천히 깨어가는 커피를 마시면서,
아주 잘 닦여진 거울로 보면 내 얼굴이
죽음 이상으로
투명해 보인다

OOH, I WANT TO ABANDON YOU

Unloaded a baggage of tepid love
he bolted me in and left
to blast free the world's dream.
I was closed again.

In the empty house I
ache in spirit,
ache in life.
Each hungry evening
my aching spirit
sits out at the doorway,
and waits to hear his footsteps
that will never return
as long as the world's dream lasts.

Ooh, I want to abandon you
I want to shed this waiting
I want to land a rich lover
I want to ready a cozy tomb

Drinking slowly intoxicating alcohol
drinking slowly detoxicating coffee, if I
gaze into a well-polished mirror, my face
appears transparent
beyond death.

첫사랑의 여자

그 여자의 몸 속에는 스물다섯에
내가 버린 童貞이 흐르고 있다.
오래 전에 떠나온 고향처럼
황량하게, 다시 늘 그리웁게.

그 여자의 두 손가락으로 쉽게 나는 열린다
무한을 향해 스스로 열리는 꽃봉우리처럼.

그 여자가 나를 만지면
스물다섯 살 적의 꿈이 깨어나
물결처럼 나를 감싼다.

이 시대의 사랑

SHE, MY FIRST LOVE

In her body flows
the virginity I deserted at twenty-five.
Like a hometown left long ago
desolately, again always yearningly.

By her two fingers I am easily opened
like a flower budding itself toward infinity.

When she touches me
my dream of twenty-five awakens
and embraces me like a wave.

가을의 끝

자 이제는 놓아버리자
우리의 메마른 신경을.
바람 저물고
풀꽃 눈을 감듯.

지난 여름 수액처럼 솟던 꿈
아직 남아도는 푸른 피와 함께
땅속으로 땅속으로
오래 전에 죽은 용암의 중심으로
부끄러움 더러움 모두 데리고
터지지 않는 그 울음 속
한 점 무늬로 사라져야겠네.

END OF AUTUMN

Let's ease now
our desiccated nerves.
As winds subside,
as wildflowers close their eyes.

With the dream surging like sap last summer
with its green blood still teeming
to the ground to the ground
to the center of long dead lava
carry all shame all filth
we shall fade as a single-dot
into that unexploding cry.

이제 나의 사랑은

종기처럼 나의 사랑은 곪아
이제는 터지려 하네.
메스를 든 당신들.
그 칼 그림자를 피해 내 사랑은
뒷전으로만 맴돌다가
이제는 어둠 속으로 숨어
종기처럼 문둥병처럼
짓물러 터지려 하네.

MY LOVE IS ABOUT TO

Festering like a boil
my love is about to burst.
You people with scalpels.
To escape those knife-shadows
lingering only along the peripheries
and now hiding in the darkness,
overripe like a boil like leprosy
my love is about to burst.

장마

넋 없이 뼈 없이
비가 온다
빗물보다 빗소리가 먼저
江을 이룬다
허공을 나직히 흘러가는
빗소리의 강물
내 늑골까지 죽음의 문턱까지
비가 내린다
물의 房에 누워
나의 꿈도 떠내려간다

RAINY SEASON

Without a soul without a bone
rain comes.
Rainsound forms a river
ahead of rainwater—
flowing softly in the empty air
the rainsound river.
To my ribs to the threshold of death
rain pours down.
Lying in the room of water
my dream too drifts away.

허공의 여자

나의 꿈속은 바람 부는 무법천지
그 누가 부르겠는가
막막 무심중에 떠 있는 나를.

다가오지 마라!
내 슬픔의 장칼(長劍)에
아무도 다가오지 마라.
내가 버리고 싶은 것은
오직 나 자신일 뿐……

하늘의 망루 위에
내 기다림을 세워놓고
시간이여 나를 눕혀라
바람 부는 허공의 침상 위에
머리는 이승의 꿈속에 처박은 채
두 발은 저승으로 뻗은 채.

이 시대의 사랑

☐☐☐ | ☐☐☐

WOMAN IN THE EMPTY AIR

Inside my dream is a lawless windy world.
Who would ever call me
afloat in this vast detachment.

Do not come near!
No one comes near
my long sword of sadness.
The one I wish to finish
is none but myself ...

Station my waiting
on a sentry in the sky
Dear Time, lay me down
on a windy bed in the empty air leaving
my head plunged into this world's dream,
my two feet stretched toward that world.

술독에 빠진 그리움

무수한 꿈이 그녀를 짓밟았다
독한 희망에 그녀는 썩어갔다
그리고 오늘밤 또다시 바람은
하늘 밖에서 그녀를 부르고
오오 벼락치는 그리움에
절망이 번개 광선처럼
그녀의 뇌 속에 침투한다
그녀의 머리통이 깨어지고
꿈이 좌르르 쏟아진다
뇌수와 함께.

이 시대의 사랑

YEARNING FALLEN INTO A KEG

Numerous dreams trampled her
Noxious hopes rotted her
Yet again tonight the wind
calls her from outside the sky
oh-oh, with thunderbolts of longing
lightning-like despair
penetrates her brain
Her head breaks open
and dreams pour clattering out
along with her brain.

사랑하는 손

거기서 알 수 없는 비가 내리지
내려서 적셔주는 가여운 안식
사랑한다고 너의 손을 잡을 때
열 손가락에 걸리는 존재의 쓸쓸함
거기서 알 수 없는 비가 내리지
내려서 적셔주는 가여운 평화

이 시대의 사랑

⬚⬚⬛ | ⬛⬚⬚

LOVING HANDS

There falls unfathomable rain
Falls and moistens the piteous solace
With words of love when I hold your hand
suspending from ten fingers the loneliness of being
There falls unfathomable rain
Falls and moistens the piteous peace

이 시대의 사랑

불러도 삼월에는 주인이 없다
동대문 발치에서 풀잎이 비밀에 젖는다.

늘 그대로의 길목에서 집으로
우리는 익숙하게 빠져들어
세상 밖의 잠속으로 내려가고
꿈의 깊은 늪 안에서 너희는 부르지만
애인아 사천 년 하늘 빛이 무거워
<이 강산 낙화유수 흐르는 물에>
우리는 발이 묶인 구름이다.

밤마다 복면한 바람이
우리를 불러내는
이 무렵의 뜨거운 암호를
죽음이 죽음을 따르는
이 시대의 무서운 사랑을
우리는 풀지 못한다

LOVE OF THIS AGE

Though you call out, there's no master in March.
At the foot of the Great East Gate[7] grass steeps in secrets.

Round the unchanging street corners
into the houses we habitually slip
into the sleep outside the world
and though you all call out from the deep swamp
     of dreams,
my beloved, by the "fallen blossoms and flowing water
     of this land"[8]
heavy with the hue of a four-thousand-year-old sky
we are ankle-shackled clouds.

The burning code of this time
the masked wind
calls us out with nightly;
the chilling love of this age
for which death follows death
—these we cannot decipher.

---

[7] During the Choson dynasty (1392–1910), the Great East Gate, or Dong-dae-mun, was the major eastern gate in the wall that surrounded Seoul. It was originally named Heung-in-ji-mun, the "Gate of Rising Benevolence," but after the students' movement on June 10, 1926, for national independence against the Japanese occupation, the Japanese renamed it Dong-dae-mun in 1934. In 1963 the gate was designated a national treasure, and since 1996 it has been called by its original name.

[8] This line is from *Nak-hwa-you-su,* which some consider to be Korea's first pop song. The song expressed youthful dreams and romances that bloom in spring as well as the pain and futility of life in turbulent times. Originally it was the theme song of a silent movie of the same title but the lyrics were rewritten several times. Because one of these rewritings was the work of poet and lyricist Jo Myongam, who went to North Korea during the Korean War, the song was completely banned from 1965 to 1987 as a result of the infamous "Popular Music Purifying Measures" passed by President Park Chung-hee.

자화상

나는 아무의 제자도 아니며
누구의 친구도 못 된다.
잡초나 늪 속에서 나쁜 꿈을 꾸는
어둠의 자손, 암시에 걸린 육신.

어머니 나는 어둠이에요.
그 옛날 아담과 이브가
풀섶에서 일어난 어느 아침부터
긴 몸뚱아리의 슬픔이에요.

밝은 거리에서 아이들은
새처럼 지저귀며
꽃처럼 피어나며
햇빛 속에 저 눈부신 天性의 사람들
저이들이 마시는 순순한 술은
갈라진 이 혀끝에는 맞지 않는구나.
잡초나 늪 속에 온몸을 사려감고
내 슬픔의 毒이 전신에 발효하길 기다릴 뿐

뱃속의 아이가 어머니의 사랑을 구하듯
하늘 향해 몰래몰래 울면서
나는 태양에의 사악한 꿈을 꾸고 있다.

이 시대의 사랑

SELF-PORTRAIT

I am nobody's pupil
nor could I be anybody's friend.
Having nightmares in weeds or swamps
a descendent of darkness, a hypnotized body.

Mother, I am the darkness.
The long-bodied sadness
ever since that morning when
Adam and Eve rose from the grass.

Kids on the bright street
chirp like birds,
bloom like flowers,
people in the sun with their dazzling nature—
yet their gentle drinks
disagree with this forked tongue.
Coiling in weeds or swamps, only waiting
for this venom of sorrow to ferment through my body.

As a fetus seeks its mother's love
shedding secret tears toward the sky
I dream a wicked dream against the sun.

만리포 마카로니 웨스턴

원주민이 떠나간 구석의 거리
주인 없는 개들이 떠돌고 있다.
숨죽인 파도의 밑뿌리가
비인 집집으로 스며들고
아직도 남아 있는 지난 여름의 죄와
질척이는 모래,
마카로니 웨스턴의 거리를 지나

그러나 만리포 앞바다에서
누가 어젯밤의 꿈을 헤아릴 것인가
나의 등뒤에서 비인 집과 바람
떠도는 개들이 수상한 몸짓으로 흔들리고

나는 지금 보고 있다
큰바다의 이제 터지는 용암이
태양을 겨누어 일제히 솟구치는 것을.

죽은 기억들을 밀어내며
내 머릿속에서 뜨겁게 뛰노는 물결
해변가 쏟아지는 햇빛 속에서
배가 고파 배가 고파
만리포 큰바다와 혼자서 살아 있다

MACARONI WESTERN OF MALI ESTUARY

Around the old-fashioned streets the natives
abandoned, ownerless dogs roam.
The roots of hushed waves
seep into each empty house,
past last summer's lingering sin,
sticky sand, and
Macaroni Western streets.

Yet at the sea off Mali Estuary
who would fathom last night's dream?
Behind my back empty houses, winds and
roaming dogs sway with suspicious motions.

And now I see
the great sea's just-exploding lava
soaring up all at once aiming at the sun.

Pushing out the dead memories
romping hot in my head, the waves
at the seashore in the shower of sunshine
Hungry Hungry
alive alone with the great sea off Mali Estuary.

---

⁹ In the mid-1960s, Italian and Spanish film producers and directors collaborated on many low-budget Westerns. These films were known as "Spaghetti Westerns" in America, but in Japan, Korea and much of Asia they were known as "Macaroni Westerns."

너에게

마음은 바람보다 쉽게 흐른다.
너의 가지 끝을 어루만지다가
어느새 나는 네 심장 속으로 들어가
영원히 죽지 않는 태풍의 눈이 되고 싶다.

□□□ | □□□

TO YOU

Mind flows easier than wind.
After caressing the tip of your branch,
slipping unnoticed into your heart, I yearn
to turn into the ever-undying eye of the storm.

불안

깊은 밤 하늘 위로
숨죽이며 다가오는 삿대 소리.
보이지 않는 허공에서
죽음이 나를 겨누고 있다.
어린 꿈들이 풀숲으로 잠복한다.
풀잎이 일시에 흔들리며
끈끈한 액체를 분비한다.
별들이 하얀 식은땀을 흘리기 시작한다.
쨍! 죽음이 나를 향해 발사한다.
두 귀로 넘쳐오는 사물의 파편들.
어둠의 아가리가 잠시 너풀거리고
보라! 까마귀 살점처럼 붉은 달이
허공을 흔들고 있다.

이 시대의 사랑

APPREHENSION

Coming from the deep night sky above,
a hushed pole-boat sound.
From invisible empty air
death aims at me.
Youthful dreams slink away in the grass.
Rustling at once,
grasses excrete sticky liquid.
Stars start to shed white cold-sweat.
Bang! Death shoots at me.
Shards of matter flooding over my ears.
The mouth of darkness flutters for a moment.
Look! The moon as red as crows' flesh
shakes the empty air.

끊임없이 나를 찾는 전화벨이 울리고

많은 사람들이 흘러갔다.
욕망과 욕망의 찌꺼기인 슬픔을 등에 얹고
그들은 나의 창가를 스쳐 흘러갔다.
나는 흘러가지 않았다.

나는 흘러가지 않았다.
열망과 허망을 버무려
나는 하루를 생산했고
일 년을 생산했고
죽음의 월부금을 꼬박꼬박 지불했다.

그래, 끊임없이 나를 호출하는 전화벨이 울리고
나는 피해가고 싶지 않았다.
그 구덩이에 내가 함몰된다 하더라도
나는 만져보고 싶었다,
운명이여.

그러나 또한 끊임없이 나는 문을 닫아걸었고
귀와 눈을 닫아걸었다.
나는 철저한 조건반사의 기계가 되어
아침엔 밥을 부르고
저녁엔 잠을 쑤셔넣었다.

(계속)

이 시대의 사랑

⊡⊡■ | ■⊡⊡

THE PHONE RANG ENDLESSLY TO FIND ME

Many people drifted away.
With desire and its residual sadness on their backs
they drifted past my window.
I did not drift away.

I did not drift away.
Mixing zeal and deceit, I
produced a day,
produced a year,
faithfully paid death monthly installments.

Yes, the phone rang endlessly to summon me
and I did not want to evade it.
Even if I were to sink into that hole
I wanted to touch it,
oh fate.

Yet again I constantly locked the door,
I locked my eyes and ears.
Becoming an inerrant conditioned-reflex machine, I
craved food in the morning,
crammed sleep in the evening.

(continued)

(끊임없이 나를 찾는 전화벨이 울리고)

궁창의 빈터에서 거대한 허무의 기계를 가동시키는
하늘의 키잡이 늙은 니힐리스트여,
당신인가 나인가
누가 먼저 지칠 것인가
(물론 나는 그 결과를 알고 있다.
내가 당신을 창조했다는 것까지)

끊임없이 나를 찾는 전화벨이 울리고
그 전화선의 마지막 끝에 동굴 같은
썩은 늪 같은 당신의 口腔이 걸려 있었다.
어느 날 그곳으로부터 죽음은
결정적으로 나를 호명할 것이고
나는 거기에 결정적으로 응답하리라.
타들어가는 내 운명의 도화선이
당신의 썩은 口腔 안에서 폭발하리라.
삼십 년 전부터 다만 헛되이,
헛되고 헛됨을 완성하기 위하여.

늙은 니힐리스트, 당신은 피묻은 너털웃음을 한 번 날리고
그 노후의 몸으로 또다시 고요히
허무의 기계를 돌리기 시작하리라.
몇 천 년 전부터 다만 헛되이,
헛되고 헛됨을 다 이루었다고 말하기 위하여.

(The Phone Rang Endlessly to Find Me)

Operating a massive nothingness machine in
    a vacant tract of blue sky,
a helmsman of the sky, oh old nihilist,
will it be you or me
who wearies first?
(Of course I know the outcome
down to the fact that I created you.)

The phone rang endlessly to find me
and at the end of that line hung
your cavernous swamp-rotten mouth.
From there someday death will
irrevocably call me by name
and I will irrevocably answer it.
The burning fuse of my fate
will explode in your rotten mouth.
Since thirty years ago only in vain,
only to fulfill the futile futility.

Old nihilist, you will toss one bloody boisterous laugh
and then again quietly with that decrepit body
start to spin the nothingness machine.
Since thousands of years ago only in vain,
only to say that all the futile futility is fulfilled.

나날

눈알을 앞으로 달고 있어도
눈알을 뒤로 바꾸어 달아도
약속된 비전은 나타나지 않고

창가의 별이 쉬임 없이 늙어간다.
치아 끝이 자꾸 바스러져 나간다.
날마다 신부들은 무덤으로 떠나가고
날마다 앞 못 보는 아기들이 한 트럭씩 태어나고
느리고 더딘 미끄러짐이 시작된다.

어둠의 볼륨을 좀더 높여라.
날마다의 커피에 증오의 독을 조금씩 더 치고
그래 그래 치정처럼 집요하게 우리는
죽음의 확실한 모습을 기다리고

그러나 냉동된 달빛 뚝뚝 떨어져 꽂히고
벽시계 과앙과앙 울리고
스틱을 든 불길한 검은 신사가
마지막 문간에 나타날 때
우리는 허리 짤린 개미떼처럼 황급히 흩어져
습기찬 잠의 굴속으로 기어내려간다.

이 시대의 사랑

EACH DAY

Whether we keep our eyeballs in front
or switch them around to hang in back
the promised vision has yet to come.

Stars by the window age restlessly.
Peaks of teeth crumble ceaselessly.
Each day brides depart for the tombs
each day blind babies are born by the truckload
and a slow sluggish sliding begins.

Turn up the darkness a little.
Spice up bit by bit the daily coffee with hate-poison.
And yes, yes, as if amorously obsessed
we stubbornly await the definite shape of death.

Yet, when the frozen moonbeams stab down
when the wall-clocks clang on
when an ominous dark gentleman
appears at the last doorway with his cane,
scattering hastily like a bisected ant train
we crawl down into the damp cave of sleep.

지금 내가 없는 어디에서

(불길해. 오늘밤 달빛이 불길해.
우리 엄마 자궁 속에 검붉은 암 기운이 번지나봐.
나 돌아가야 할 곳이 흔들려, 자꾸만 물결쳐.)

지금 내가 없는 어디에서
내 친구는 내 친구의 친구와 히히덕거리고

지금 내가 없는 어디에서
내 애인은 내 애인의 애인과 놀아나고

지금 내가 없는 어디에서 죽음은
내가 있는 곳으로 눈길을 돌리기 시작한다.

도망갈 수 없어 ! 도망가지 못해 !

내 머리통은 온 아랫목을 헤매며
으으…… 즈즈…… 으깨진 무선기처럼 신음하고
남편아 네 두 손을 다고
아내야 네 두 팔을 다고,
죽음의 눈빛은 깊고도 깊어
으으…… 즈즈……
이승의 지푸라기라도 한 가닥 건네다오.

이 시대의 사랑

⸳◻◼ │ ◼⸳◻⸳

SOMEWHERE WITHOUT ME NOW

(Ominous. Moonlight tonight is ominous.
The crimson metastasis of cancer must be spreading in
    my mom's womb.
Where I shall return quakes, constantly undulates.)

Somewhere without me now
my friend frolics with my friend's friend,

somewhere without me now
my lover flirts with my lover's lover,

somewhere without me now death
begins to turn its eyes toward me.

Impossible to run away! Unable to run away!

Hovering all over the floor, my skull
uhh … tzz … moans like a crushed walkie-talkie,
oh husband, give me your hands,
oh wife, give me your arms,
deep and deep is the gaze of death
uhh … tzz …
please toss me at least a straw of this life.

□■□ | ■□■

197X년의 우리들의 사랑
─아무도 그 시간의 火傷을 지우지 못했다

　몇 년 전, 제기동 거리엔 건조한 먼지들만 횡행했고
우리는 언제나 우리가 아니었다. 우리는 언제나 잠들어 있거나
취해 있거나 아니면 시궁창에 빠진 해진 신발짝
처럼 더러운 물결을 따라 하염없이 흘러가고 있었고…
…제대하여 복학한 늙은 학생들은 아마 여자하고나 장
가가버리고 사학년 계집아이들은 아무 남자하고나 약혼
해버리고 착한 아이들은 알맞은 향기를 내뿜으며 시들어
갔다.

(계속)

　　　　　　　　　　　이 시대의 사랑

⊡⊡■ | ■⊡⊡

OUR LOVE IN 197X[10]

—NO ONE COULD ERASE THE BURN-MARKS OF THAT TIME.

Years ago, nothing but arid dust blew rampant over
the streets of Jegi Village, and we were never ourselves.
We were always either asleep, or drunk, or drifted
aimlessly upon the dirty waves like tattered shoes
flushed into a ditch ... Discharged from mandatory
military service, the older male students got married off
to any woman, and the senior girls got engaged to any
man, and the good kids withered, emitting proper
scents.

(continued)

---

[10] In her essay, "Yang-cheol-buk Yougam [Regret about The Tin Drum]"
(from her essay collection entitled Han Ge-eureun Si-inui Iyagi [One Lazy Poet's
Story], Chaek-sesang Press: 1989, p. 135), Choi stated that "Love of This Age" was
written in 1975, and that "Our Love in 197X" poem was written to commemorate
that year. This was the year Korea University—where Choi attended was—shut
down to squelch widespread student protests against military rule and undemo-
cratic constitutional changes. When the protests spread to other campuses across
the nation, President Park arrested over 1,000 people. On April 10, less than a day
after Park's military regime sentenced eight leaders to death on the charges of agi-
tating under North Korean orders, Park executed them and cremated their bodies
immediately to hide evidence of torture. (Cited from *Sabeob-Sarin: 1975-nyeon
Saworui Hakssa*l [Judicial killings: April 1975 Massacre], eds. Catholic Human
Rights Committee, Hangmin Press, 2001.)

□□□ | □□□

(197X년의)

　그해 늦가을과 초겨울 사이, 우리의 노쇠한 혈관을 타
고 그리움의 피는 흘렀다. 그리움의 어머니는 마른 강줄
기, 술과 불이 우리를 불렀다. 향유 고래 울음 소리 같
은 밤 기적이 울려퍼지고 개처럼 우리는 제기동 빈 거리
를 헤맸다. 눈알을 한없이 굴리면서 꿈속에서도 행진해 나갔다.
때로 골목마다에서 진짜 개들이 기총소사하듯 짖어대곤 했다.
그러나 197X년, 우리들 꿈의 오합지졸
들이 제아무리 집중사격을 가해도 현실은 요지부동이었
다. 우리의 총알은 언제나 절망만으로 만들어진것이었
으므로……

　어느덧 방학이 오고 잠이 오고 깊은 눈이 왔을 때 제기동 거리는
"미안해, 사랑해"라는 말로 진흙탕을 이루
었고 우리는 잠 속에서도 "사랑해, 죽여줘"라고 잠꼬대
를 했고 그때마다 마른 번개 사이로 그리움의 어머니는 야윈 팔을
치켜들고 나직히 말씀하였다. "세상의 아들아
내 손이 비었구나, 너희에게 줄 게 아무것도 없구나."
그리고 우리는 정말로 개처럼 납작하게 엎드려 고요히 침을 흘리며
죽어갔다.

　　　　　　　　　　　이 시대의 사랑

(Our Love in 197X)

Between that late fall and early winter, the blood of yearning flowed through our decrepit veins. The mother of yearning was a dried riverbed, alcohol and fire called us. The night siren echoed like a sperm whale's cry, and like dogs, we roamed along the empty streets of Jegi Village. Restlessly rolling our eyes, we marched on even in our dreams. At times from each and every alley the real dogs barked like firing machine guns. But in 197X, however assiduously our dream-rabble fired, reality was unyielding. For our bullets were made always and only of despair ...

When vacation and sleep and deep snow came unawares, the streets of Jegi Village got muddied with "Sorry, love you" and even in our sleep we murmured "Love you, kill me" and each time between dry thunders the mother of yearning spoke low with her emaciated arms raised. "Sons of the world, my hands are empty, I have nothing to give you." And truly like dogs, lying flat face down and drooling silently, our dying began.

오늘 저녁이 먹기 싫고

오늘 저녁이 먹기 싫고 내일 아침이 살기 싫으니
이대로 쓰러져 잠들리라,
쥐도새도모르게 잠들어버리리라.
그러나 자고 싶어도 죽고 싶어도
누울 곳 없는 정신은 툭하면 집을 나서서
이 거리 저 골목을 기웃거리고,
살코기처럼 흥건하게 쏟아지는 불빛들.
오오 그대들 오늘도 살아 계신가,
정처없이 살아 계신가.
밤나무 이파리 실뱀처럼 뒤엉켜
밤꽃들 불을 켜는 네온의 집 창가에서
나는 고아처럼 바라본다.
일촉즉발의 사랑 속에서 따스하게 숨쉬는 염통들,
구름처럼 부풀어오른 애인들의 배를 베고
여자들 남자들 하염없이 평화롭게 붕붕거리지만
흐흥 뭐해서 뭐해, 별들은 매연에 취해 찔끔거리고
구슬픈 밤공기가 이별의 닐리리를 불러대는 밤거리.
올 늦가을엔 새빨간 루즈를 칠하고
내년엔 실한 아들 하나 낳을까
아니면 내일부터 단식을 시작할까
그러나 돌아와 방문을 열면
응답처럼 보복처럼, 나의 기둥서방
죽음이 나보다 먼저 누워
두 눈을 멀뚱거리고 있다.

NO APPETITE FOR TONIGHT'S DINNER

No appetite for dinner tonight, no will to face tomorrow
    morning,
so I will fall and sleep as I am,
letnoratsnobirdsknow, I will just fall asleep.
Hoping to sleep, hoping to die, yet with nowhere to lie,
my spirit often steps out of its house
snoops around this street or that alley where
beams of lights pouring down like succulent flesh.
Oh-oh darlings, are you still alive today,
are you aimlessly alive?
By the window of the neon house where chestnut flowers
light up like threadsnakes entangled with
        chestnut leaves,
I gaze on like an orphan.
With warmly breathing hearts in peevish love
though women and men buzz peacefully evermore,
pillowing on lovers' bellies swollen like clouds,
ho-hum, what's the use, on the streets smog-drunk stars
        exude tears,
melancholy night air croons farewell songs.
Shall I put on hot-red lipstick this late fall
and give birth to a healthy son next year
or shall I begin fasting from tomorrow?
But when I return and open the door
as if in answer, as if in retaliation, my pimp
death lies ahead of me
vacantly blinking his eyes.

그리하여 어느 날, 사랑이여

한 숟갈의 밥, 한 방울의 눈물로
무엇을 채울 것인가,
밥을 눈물에 말아먹는다 한들.

그대가 아무리 나를 사랑한다고 해도
혹은 내가 아무리 그대를 사랑한다고 해도
나는 오늘의 닭고기를 씹어야 하고
나는 오늘의 눈물을 삼켜야 한다.
그러므로 이제 비유로써 말하지 말자.
모든 것은 콘크리트처럼 구체적이고
모든 것은 콘크리트 벽이다.
비유가 아니라 주먹이며,
주먹의 바스러짐이 있을 뿐,

이제 이룰 수 없는 것을 또한 이루려 하지 말며
헛되고 헛됨을 다 이루었다고도 말하지 말며

가거라, 사랑인지 사람인지,
사랑한다는 것은 너를 위해 죽는 게 아니다.
사랑한다는 것은 너를 위해
살아,
기다리는 것이다,
다만 무참히 꺾여지기 위하여.

(계속)

이 시대의 사랑

THEREFORE SOMEDAY, LOVE

With a spoonful of rice, with a single teardrop,
what could you fill,
even if you gulp the rice mixed with that teardrop?

No matter how much you love me
no matter how much I love you
I have to chew today's chicken
I have to swallow today's tear.
Therefore, let's just stop speaking in metaphors.
Everything is tangible as concrete
everything is a concrete wall.
Not a metaphor but a fist,
nothing but a crumbling fist exists.

Also, let's just stop venturing what cannot be fulfilled,
let's stop claiming to have fulfilled all futile futilities.

Leave me, love or lover,
to love is not to die for you.
To love is but
to wait for you
alive,
only to be mercilessly broken.

(continued)

(그리하여 어느 날, 사랑이여)

그리하여 어느 날 사랑이여,
내 몸을 분질러다오.
내 팔과 다리를 꺾어

네

꽃
병
에

꽂
아
다
오

이 시대의 사랑

■ ■ ■ | ■ ■ ■

(Therefore Someday, Love)

Therefore someday, love,
break my body.
Crack my arms and legs,

s
t
i
c
k

t
h
e
m

i
n

y
o
u
r

v
a
s
e

□■□ │ ■□■

주인 없는 잠이 오고

주인 없는 잠이 오고
잠 없는 밤이 다시 헤매고,
애들아, 이게 詩냐 막걸리냐,
겨울에 마신 술이
봄에 취하고
흘러간다 흘러가서.

나를 붙잡지 마라,
나는 네 에미가 아니다,
네 새끼도 아니다.

오냐 나 혼자 간다 가마,
늙은 몸이 詩투성이 피투성이로.
환히 불 밝혀진 고층 건물
층층이 밝은 물이 찰랑거리고
아직은 아직은이라고 말하며
희망은 뱃가죽이 땅가죽이 되도록 기어나가고
어느 날 나는 나의 무덤에 닿을 것이다.
棺 속에서 행복한 구더기들을 키우며
비로소 말갛게 깨어나
홀로 노래 부르기 시작할 것이다.

이 시대의 사랑

⊡⊡■ | ■⊡⊡

HERE COMES OWNERLESS SLEEP

Here comes ownerless sleep
and a sleepless night wanders again—
Hey kids, is this a poem or rice wine?
Alcohol consumed in winter
gets me tipsy in spring
and it flows and flows ...

Don't hold me back,
I'm not your mommy
nor am I your kid.

Surely, I'll go, I'll go alone,
old body soaked with blood soaked with poems.
Of a brightly lit skyscraper
vivacious water sloshes on each floor
and saying not yet, not yet,
hope crawls out grating its gut into the earth
and someday I will reach my tomb.
Growing happy maggots in my casket
only then, will I sober up lucid
and alone, start to sing.

한 목소리가

한 목소리가 허공에 숨어 있다.
눈빛을 반짝이며 십 년을
숨어 떠돌던 목소리,
언젠가 누군가의 베개맡에서
사랑해라고 말했던 목소리.

이윽고 말갛게 씻겨져 나간
백골의 추억으로 그대는 일어선다.
그대의 비인 두 눈구멍을 뚫고
두 줄기의 바람이 불어간다.

뼈의 기타 가락이 별빛처럼 부서지며
별빛 같은 물이 흘러나오고
한번 스쳐가는 바람의 활에도
석회질의 추억은 맑게 울리며
홀로 노래하기 시작한다.

바다 위의 내 집에는
흰 파도의 침실이 하나……

이 시대의 사랑

⊡▪◼ | ◼▪⊡

A VOICE

A voice is hiding in the empty air.
The voice lurked wandering for ten years
with sparks in its eyes,
the voice once whispered I love you
near someone's pillow.

Finally you arise as the memory
of white bone washed clean.
Through your hollow eyesockets
two windstreams flow.

Like starlight guitar melody of the bone shatters,
like starlight water streams out
and even with a single passing plectrum of wind
the calcified memory keenly resonates
and alone, starts to sing.

> In my house on the sea
> I have one bedroom for white waves …

내가 너를 너라고 부를 수 없는 곳에서

1

어느 한 순간 세계의 모든 음모가
한꺼번에 불타오르고
우연히 발을 잘못 디딜 때
터지는 지뢰처럼
꿈도 도처에서 폭발한다.

삼억 이천만 원짜리 선글래스를 낀 것은 그젯밤의 꿈,

어두운 밝음 속에서
우리가 서로를 껴안은 것은
어젯밤의 꿈,

네가 떠나고
바람 불고
내가 죽는 것은
오늘 한낮의 꿈.

2

또다시 한 세월이 끝났을 때
나의 무릎은 절단되어 있었고
너의 문은 닫혀 있었다.

네가 없는 그 거리,
나침반이, 운명 지침서가 헛돌고
한 평생이, 온 인류가 헛돌고

(계속)

이 시대의 사랑

WHERE I CANNOT CALL YOU YOU

1

At one moment all together
every plot in the world flares up
and dreams too explode everywhere
like landmines blowing up
after an accidental misstep.

Wearing million-dollar sunglasses is the day before
    yesterday's dream,

us embracing each other
in the obscure brightness
is yesterday's dream,

your leaving,
wind blowing,
my dying
is this midday's dream.

2

When again one era was over
my knees were severed
and your doors were shut.

On that street without you,
a compass, a guide to fate idly spun,
a lifetime, all mankind idly spun,

(continued)

(내가 너를 너라고 부를 수 없는 곳에서)

헛도는 그 깊이로
흩어져내리는 내 꽁지의
마지막 깃털이 보였다.

3

내가 너를 너라고 부를 수 없는 곳에서
흐르는 물은 흐름을 정지하고

이제 눈감는 자는 영원히
다시 눈떠 헤매지 않으리니

말없이 한 여자가 떠나가고
바다의 회색 철문이 닫혀진다.

⊡⊡◼ | ◼⊡⊡

(Where I Cannot Call You You)*

and deep down that vortex of idle spinning
I saw the last feather
of my scattering tail fall.

3

Where I cannot call you *you*
flowing water will halt its flow

and ones who close their eyes now
will never open them again to wander.

A woman departs without a word
and the sea's gray iron gate shuts.

너는 즐거웠었니

네가 나를 차버렸을 때
너는 즐거웠었니,
내 사랑 내 아가야,

어느 날 네가 병든 낙엽처럼
내 문간에 불려 떨어진다면
어느 날 네가 허깨비처럼
내 창가에 돌아와 선다면

네가 쓰러지기 전에
먼저 나를 차주지 않겠니,

다시는 내가 이 세상에 기어나오지 못하도록
모가지를 꿈틀거리며 기어나오지 못하도록
네가 쓰러지기 전에
먼저 나를 차주지 않겠니,
다정한 내 사랑 내 아가야.

가여운 내 사랑 내 아가야!

이 시대의 사랑

· □ ■ | ■ □ ·

WERE YOU HAPPY?

When you abandoned me
were you happy,
my love, my baby?

If someday you are blown like a sick leaf
and land on my doorstep
if someday you return like a phantom
and stand by my window

before you collapse
won't you first give me a kick?

Never to crawl out again into this world,
never to crawl out wriggling my neck,
before you collapse
won't you first give me a kick,
my sweet love, my baby?

My poor love, my baby!

■■■ **II** ■■■

기억의 집

HOUSE OF MEMORY

봄

동의하지 않아도
봄은 온다.
삼십삼 세 미혼 고독녀의 봄
실업자의 봄
납세 의무자의 봄.

봄에는 산천초목이 되살아나고
쓰레기들도 싱싱하게 자라나고
삼킬 수도 뱉을 수도 없이
내 입안에서 오물이 자꾸 커간다.
믿을 수 없이, 기적처럼, 벌써
터널만큼 늘어난 내 목구멍 속으로
쉴 새 없이 덤프 트럭이 들어와
플라스틱과 고철과 때와 땀과 똥을
쿵 하고 부려놓고 가고

내 주여 네 때가 가까왔나이다
이 말도 나는 발음하지 못하고
다만 오물로 가득 찬 내 아가리만
찢어질 듯 터져내릴 듯
허공에 둥둥 떠 있다.

□□□ ‖ □□□

SPRING

Seeking no consent
spring comes.
The spring of a thirty-three-year-old spinster
the spring of a laid-off worker
the spring of a taxpayer.

In spring all nature revives
even trash revivifies
and unable to swallow or spit
the muck in my mouth grows relentlessly.
Incredibly, miraculously, into my throat
already stretched wide as a tunnel
dump-trucks incessantly come and go
dumping thump
plastics, iron-scraps, scum, sweat and shit.

My Jesus, your time is near—
unable to utter even these words,
only my muck-filled maw alone
floats buoyantly in the empty air
about to rip, about to pop.

내게 새를 가르쳐 주시겠어요?

내게 새를 가르쳐 주시겠어요?
그러면 내 심장 속 새 집의 열쇠를 빌려드릴게요.

내 몸을 맑은 시냇물 줄기로 휘감아 주시겠어요?
그러면 난 당신 몸 속을 작은 조약돌로 굴러다닐게요.

내 텃밭에 심을 푸른 씨앗이 되어 주시겠어요?
그러면 난 당신 창가로 기어올라 빨간 깨꽃으로
까꿍! 피어날게요.

엄하지만 다정한 내 아빠가 되어 주시겠어요?
그러면 난 너그럽고 순한 당신의 엄마가 돼드릴게요.

오늘밤 내게 단 한 번의 깊은 입맞춤을 주시겠어요?
그러면 내일 아침에 예쁜 아이를 낳아드릴게요.

그리고 어느 저녁 늦은 햇빛에 실려
내가 이 세상을 떠나갈 때에,
저무는 산그림자보다 기인 눈빛으로
잠시만 나를 바래다 주시겠어요?

그러면 난 뭇 별들 사이에 그윽한 눈동자로 누워
밤마다 당신을 지켜봐드릴게요.

□·□ ‖ ■··

WOULD YOU TEACH ME A BIRD?

Would you teach me a bird?
Then I'd lend you the birdhouse-key in my heart.

Would you entwine my body with a crystal brook?
Then I'd roll inside your body as a tiny pebble.

Would you become a green seed to sow in
    my vegetable garden?
Then I'd crawl up to your window as a red sesame bud
and Boom! I'd bloom.

Would you be my stern yet sweet daddy?
Then I'd be your generous and gentle mommy.

Would you give me the one and only deep kiss tonight?
Then I'd deliver a pretty baby for you in the morning.

And someday wafting on late evening sunlight
as I withdraw from this world,
with a gaze longer than the dimming mountain-shadow
would you see me off just for a while?

Then reclining amongst the stars as a mystic pupil
I'd watch over you each and every night.

겨울에 바다에 갔었다

겨울에 바다에 갔었다.
갈매기들이 끼룩거리며 흰 똥을 갈기고
죽어 삼 일 간을 떠돌던 한 여자의 시체가
해양 경비대 경비정에 걸렸다.
여자의 자궁은 바다를 향해 열려 있었다.
(오염된 바다)
열려진 자궁으로부터 병약하고 창백한 아이들이
바다의 햇빛이 눈이 부셔 비틀거리며 쏟아져나왔다.
그들은 파도의 포말을 타고
오대양 육대주로 흩어져갔다.
죽은 여자는 흐물흐물한 빈 껍데기로 남아
비닐처럼 떠돌고 있었다.
세계 각처로 뿔뿔이 흩어져간 아이들은
남아연방의 피터마릿츠버그나 오덴달루스트에서
질긴 거미집을 치고, 비율빈의 정글에서
땅속에다 알을 까놓고 독일의 베를린이나
파리의 오르샹 가나 오스망 가에서
야밤을 틈타 매독을 퍼뜨리고 사생아를 낳으면서,
간혹 너무도 길고 지루한 밤에는 혁명을 일으킬 것이다.
언제나 불발의 혁명을.
겨울에 바다에 갔었다.
(오염된 바다)

기억의 집

□□■ ‖ ■□■

I WENT TO THE SEA IN WINTER

I went to the sea in winter.
Honking seagulls shot white shit
and a coast-guard boat caught a woman's corpse
that had floated for three days.
Her womb was open toward the sea.
(The polluted sea.)
Pale sickly kids poured from her open womb
staggering blinded by the sun's sea-glare.
Riding on wave-froth
they dispersed to the five oceans and six continents.
Left behind as flabby empty skin
the dead woman floated like plastic.
Dispersed to every nook of the world, the kids will
spin strong spiderwebs in Pietermaritzburg
    or in Odendaalsrustin, South Africa,
hatch eggs on the jungle floor in the Philippines,
spread syphilis and beget bastards
under deep-night cover in Berlin, Germany
or on Rue d'Orchien or on Boulevard Haussmann
    in Paris—
occasionally on nights too long or dull the kids will
    ignite revolutions.
Forever misfiring revolutions.
I went to the sea in winter.
(The polluted sea.)

폰 가갸 씨의 肖像

9시, 사무실 출입문이 폰 가갸 씨를 기운차게 연다.
의자가 걸어와 폰 가갸 씨 위에 앉는다
볼펜이 그의 손가락을 꼬나쥐고
활자들이 그를 꼬나보기 시작한다.

12시, 점심이 그를 잘도 먹어치우고
때가 되면 오줌이 유유하게 그를 갈긴다.
때때로 심심해서 전화가 자꾸 그를 걸어본다.
여보십니까? 여보십시다! (존재의 딸꾹질)
시간이 가기도 하고 안 가기도 하면서
이윽고 월급봉투가 그를 호주머니에 쑤셔넣는다.
6시 반, 54번 버스가 다시 폰 가갸 씨를 올라탄다.
원효대교가 다시 홀라당 그를 넘어간다.

현관문이 그를 열고 집어 넣는다.
따뜻한 방바닥이 그를 때려눕힌다.
잠이 아작아작 그를 갉아먹기 시작한다.
그러나 이윽고!
꿈속에서 대한민국이 열렬하게 그를 찬양하고
여의도 광장 한가운데 그의 기념비를 세운다.
코러스도 웅장하게 울려퍼지며
우러러 찬미할지어다!

⬚⬚■ ‖ ■⬚⬚

PORTRAIT OF MR. PHON GA-GYA

9 a.m., the office door forcefully opens Mr. Phon Ga-gya.[11]
The chair walks over and sits on Mr. Phon Ga-gya.
The pen twists his fingers,
and the printouts start to glare at him cynically.

12 p.m., lunch gobbles him up pretty good
and in due course urine passes him leisurely.
Sometimes out of boredom phone calls make him repeatedly.
Hello, can you hear me? Hey, listen to me!
    (The hiccups of existence.)
Time sometimes flies and other times not,
but at last, a paycheck stuffs him into its pocket.
6:30 p.m., Bus 54 again gets on Mr. Phon Ga-gya.
Grand Wonhyo Bridge again passes quickly over him.

The front door opens him and enters.
The heated floor throws itself onto him.
Sleep starts to nibble him crunch-crunch.
But at last!
In his dream the Republic of Korea worships him fervently
and erects his monument right in the middle of the
    Yeoui Island Agora.
The chorus too echoes majestically—
Revere and Praise!

---

[11] "Phon Ga-gya": The sense of this title is difficult to determine, but we sense that "Ga-gya" suggests a reference to the Korean language. Modern Korean has fourteen consonants and ten vowels, and "ga, gya" is a combination of the first consonant and the first two vowels. Because of this order, "ga, gya" is familiar from the drills of schoolchildren first learning the alphabet. Moreover, for centuries the Korean language was known by many different names, among which was "Gagya," until the name "Hangeul" became standard early in the twentieth century.

즐거운 일기

오늘 나는 기쁘다. 어머니는 건강하심이 증명되었고
밀린 번역료를 받았고 낮의 어느 모임에서 수수한 남자 를
소개받았으므로.

오늘도 여의도 강변에선 날개들이 풍선 돋친 듯 팔렸
고 도곡동 개나리 아파트의 밤하늘에선 달님이 별님들을
둘러앉히고 맥주 한잔씩 돌리며 봉봉 크랙카를 깨물고 잠든
기린이의 망막에선 노란 튤립 꽃들이 까르르거리고기린이
엄마의 꿈속에선 포니 자가용이 휘발유도 없이 잘 나가고
피곤한 기린이 아빠의 겨드랑이에서 지금 남몰래 일
센티미터의 날개가 돋고……

(계속)

▪▫▪ ‖ ▪▪▫

MERRY DIARY

I am happy today. My mother tested healthy
and   I received the overdue translation fee
and because I was introduced to a modest man at an
afternoon gathering.

Again today on the riverbanks of Yeoui Island, wings
were sold as if they'd grown balloons[12] and in the
night sky above Golden Bells Apartments on
Dogok Street, dear moon sits dear stars around
and treats them each   to a glass of beer and
yellow tulips giggle on the retinas of Kirin who
falls asleep nibbling a Bon-Bon cracker and in
the dream of Kirin's mom a Pinto[13] runs on with
no gas and now from the armpits of Kirin's tired
dad centimeter-long wings grow secretly ...

(continued)

[12] For things to "sell as if they'd grown wings" is the Korean expression equiv-
alent to "sell like hot cakes." In the poem Choi inverted this idiom to say that "the
wings sell as if they'd grown" other things.

[13] Choi refers here to the Hyundai Pony, a small rear-wheel-drive car pro-
duced in South Korea from 1975 to 1990. To avoid confusion with the Ford Pony
cars, which were highly styled, sporty, and performance-oriented, we referred to
the Ford "Pinto," a subcompact car produced from 1971 to 1980, the name of
which also is a type of horse.

(즐거운 일기)

수영이 삼촌 별아저씨 오늘도 캄사캄사합니다. 아저씨
들이 우리 조카들을 많이많이 사랑해주신 덕분에 오늘도
우리는 코리아의 유구한 푸른 하늘 아래 꿈 잘 꾸고 한
판 잘 놀아났습니다.
　　　　아싸라비아
　　　　도로아미타불

□■□ ‖ ■□·

(Merry Diary)

Uncle Su-young, Uncle Star,[14] thank you thank you again. Owing to your immense love, we, your nephews, dreamed big again today and had a grand spree under this everlasting blue sky of Korea.
Assa-rabia, doro-amitabul![15]
Hurray, all back down the drain!

---

[14] "Uncle Su-young, Uncle Star": here Choi names two of the most prominent modernist poets. Kim Su-yeong (1921–1968) employed everyday language and innovations like surrealism, abstraction, prose, slang, and profanity in his poetry. He died in a traffic accident in 1968. Though only one volume of his poetry was published in 1959, his significance and impact as a poet as well as a critic on modern Korean poetry is immeasurable. The Kim Su-yeong Contemporary Poetry Award is named in his honor. "Uncle Star" refers to Jeong Hyeon-jong (1939-), a poet known for his innovative technique and philosophical depth. After his first poetry volume, Dream of an Object, in 1972, he wrote many more volumes including the one that led to his nickname, I am Uncle Star.

[15] *Assa-rabia*, translated below as "hurray," derives from *ssawoo-rabi*, "the fighter," and was used to hail the victors of wars or games. *Doro-amitabul*, translated below as "All back down the drain," originated from the Buddhist mantra *Namu-amitabul*, "Save us, merciful Buddha." But people often use *doro*, which means "waste of labor" in Chinese and "again" in Korean, when time and effort seem wasted by a trivial mistake. It expresses a comical sense for the futility in life.

여성에 관하여

여자들은 저마다의 몸 속에 하나씩의 무덤을 갖고 있다.
죽음과 탄생이 땀 흘리는 곳,
어디로인지 떠나기 위하여 모든 인간들이 몸부림치는
영원히 눈먼 항구.
알타미라 동굴처럼 거대한 사원의 폐허처럼
굳어진 죽은 바다처럼 여자들은 누워 있다.
새들의 고향은 거기.
모래바람 부는 여자들의 내부엔
새들이 최초의 알을 까고 나온 탄생의 껍질과
죽음의 잔해가 탄피처럼 가득 쌓여 있다.
모든 것들이 태어나고 또 죽기 위해선
그 폐허의 사원과 굳어진 죽은 바다를 거쳐야만 한다.

⬛ ‖ ⬛

ON WOMANHOOD

Women have one tomb each in their bodies.
Where death and birth sweat,
where all mortals writhe to depart for somewhere,
a forever-blind port.
Like Altamira caves, like giant temple ruins,
like ossified dead seas women lie.
The birthplace of birds is there.
Inside women where sandstorms blow,
the primeval birth shells and death debris of birds
pile high like empty bullet casings.
To be born and again to die, everything must
pass through those ruined temples and ossified dead
    seas.

□□□ ‖ □□□

여의도 광시곡

1

가물거리는 정신의 한 끝을 헤집고 나와
다시 다른 한 끝에서 침몰하기 위하여
원효대교, 그 허상의 다리를 넘어
섬으로 진입하는 사람들.
유해 색소의 햇빛에 조금씩 들끓으며
발효하기 시작하는 거대한 반죽 덩어리.

　　　　　　　　　　　　　　　　　—여의도는 거룩한
　　　　　　　　　　　　　　　　　　천상(天上)의 빵.

　　　　　　　　　　　　　　　(계속)

　　　　　　　　　　　　　　　기억의 집

□·■ ‖ ■·□

YEOUI ISLAND RHAPSODY

1

To burrow through and emerge at one end of a
    murky spirit,
then to submerge again at its other end,
the people who are entering the Island crossing over
Grand Wonhyo Bridge, that phantom bridge.
Boiling bit by bit in the sun's toxic pigments,
a giant lump of dough beginning to ferment.
                    —Yeoui Island[16] is the holy
                                   bread of heaven.

(continued)

---

[16] *Yeoui* means "available" or "useless." Yeouido, or Yeoui Island, was once a vacant island in Seoul's Han River that was used as a common pasture for sheep and goats. The Japanese Occupational Government constructed Seoul's first airport there in April 1924. After 1970, when a wide bridge connecting the island to the mainland was built, development of the area accelerated as part of President Park Chung-hee's Han River Development Project. Yeouido Village was formed as a separate entity in 1971, and now serves as Korea's Wall Street.

(여의도 광시곡)

2

구르는 헛바퀴의 완강한 힘, 치욕이여
중국집 짬뽕 속의 삶은 바퀴벌레여,
그래도 코를 벌름거리며
돼지들은 죽어서도 즐겁고
오, 제 먹는 게 제 살인 줄 모르는
무의식의 죄의식의 내출혈의 비몽사몽의

손들엇 탕탕!
창 밖엔 찌를 듯 환한 햇빛.
샛강 빈 벌판에서, 누가 노래 불러?
귀아리게
쟁쟁하게
불끈 솟아오르는 산들,
어린 날의 메아리가 되살아나
흐야 호 바다로 내달아
바다!

일어나!

솟구쳐!

위로

위로

정점의 피

태양

(계속)

기억의 집

⊡⊡⊡ ‖ ⊡⊡⊡

(Yeoui Island Rhapsody)

2

The stubborn force of a skidding wheel, oh Shame,
oh the stewed cockroach in Chinese noodles,
yet, quivering their nostrils
pigs are merry even after their death,
oh unaware that what one eats is one's own flesh,
unconscious, guilty, internally hemorrhaging, dazed—
                    Hands-up, bang!
          Stabbingly bright sunshine out the window.
          In the empty tributary bed, who's singing?
                    Ear-splittingly
                          ringingly
               suddenly soaring mountains,
                echoes of childhood revive,
                hurray, dash off to the sea,
                          The sea!

               Rise up!

          Soar up!

     Up

   Up

The summit of blood

The sun

(continued)

(여의도 광시곡)

3

그러나 예, 기다려야지요.
즐거운 사탕발림의 기다림.
그러나 예, 기다려야지요.
우리의 기다림에도
프리미엄이 붙을 테니까요.

오 이 느긋한 기다림의 사원에서
영원히 기다리게 하소서.
마지막 임종처럼 다가올
약속의 땅을 꿈꾸며
우리 네 활개 펴고
잠들어 있게 하소서,
지금 여기서 영원히.

(계속)

기억의 집

(Yeoui Island Rhapsody)

3

But of course, we must wait.
Merry sugarcoated waiting.
But of course, we must wait.
For our waiting also
will earn a premium.

Oh, in this temple of leisurely waiting
let us wait forever.
Dreaming of the Promised Land
that will approach us as our last mortal moment
let us stay asleep
with our four limbs spread wide,
here, now and forever.

(continued)

(여의도 광시곡)

4

시간은 저 혼자 능률 능률 흘러가고
보라, 우리의 오물더미 위에서,
구린내도 그윽한 문화의 오븐 위에서
무럭무럭 김을 풍기며
거대하게 부풀어오르는 여의도를.

　　　　　　　　　　　　　　　　-여의도는 거대한
　　　　　　　　　　　　　　　　　天上의 빵.

그윽한 향취 속에서
저는 잠든 것도 깬 것도 아니었어요.
다만 이 세상을 손수건처럼 얌전히 접어두고서
한 세월 아득히 눕고 싶었을 뿐이에요.
—그때 거기에서 많은 사람들이 울고 있었는데
　나는 왜? 알지 못했죠.
—그때 그 거리에서 검은 상복 입은 사람들이
　바다로 내닫고 있었는데
나는 왜? 알지 못했죠.

하지만 어느 순간 내 꿈을 타고 한 마리 뱀이
내 입 속으로 목구멍 속으로 들어가고
그 순간 큰골이 팽팽한 풍선처럼
내 머리 밖으로 부풀어오르고

그때 나는 보았죠.
피골이 상접한 내 정신이
땡땡 부어오른 내 육신의 관을 이끌고
대방 터널을 힘겹게 빠져나가는 것을.

　　　　　　　　　　　　　　　　　　(계속)

◨◨◨ ‖ ◨◨◨

(Yeoui Island Rhapsody)

4

Time flows apart moment by moment
and behold, on the heap of our filth,
on the stove of culture with its stink ambrosial,
densely steaming
monstrously rising, Yeoui Island.
                                —Yeoui Island is the gargantuan
                                        bread of heaven.
In the ambrosial scent
I was neither asleep nor awake.
After neatly folding this world like a handkerchief
I only wanted to lie down a lifetime apart.
—There and then, many people were weeping,
    but why? I didn't know.
—Then on that street, people in mourning black
    were dashing off to the sea,
    but why? I didn't know.

Yet suddenly a snake riding my dream
slid into my mouth, into my throat
and at once my cerebrum swelled
out of my head like a taut balloon

and then I saw
my spirit, emaciated to skin and bone,
pulling my bloated corporeal casket,
passing laboriously through Daebang Tunnel.

(continued)

(여의도 광시곡)

5

날개 돋친 듯 홰를 치며
열심히 빵을 굽는 사람들
살인적으로 미소짓는 假花들
심장과 성기와 항문을 발랑
얼굴에 달고 다니는 사람들

혹은 삶 속에 죽음의 기념비를 세우며
심장과 성기와 항문을 꼭꼭 잠그고
막대그래프처럼 걷는 사람들
차트 같은 표정의 얼굴들

옛날의 금잔디
창가에서 노래하던
처녀들의 순한 목소리 문득 그치고
수직으로 곧게 추락하는 새들.
보이지 않게 습한 기류의 이동이 시작되고
비닐조각 볼펜 서류철,
인기 가수의 사진들, 사산된 아이들이
검은 하구로 떠내려와
검은 운명을 짜맞추기 시작한다.
—각성하라
너희의 꿈을 뒤덮을
홍수가 진행되고 있다.
그리고 너희에겐 되돌아갈 땅,
세습의 땅도 없다.   (계속)

기억의 집

□□□ ‖ □□□

(Yeoui Island Rhapsody)

5

Flapping as if they'd grown wings
people who diligently bake bread
artificial flowers that murderously smile
people who go to and fro shamelessly displaying
hearts, genitals, and anuses on their faces

or erecting monuments of death in life
with tightly locking hearts, genitals, and anuses
people who walk like bar-graphs
their faces with chart-like expressions

"Golden grass of the old days"[17]
the gentle singing of virgins by a window
suddenly stops,
and vertically plunging birds.
Invisibly the humid airstream begins to shift
and plastic scraps, pens, files,
pop-singers' photos, aborted babies
drift down to the black river mouth
and begin to assemble black fate.
—Awake!
   The flood is advancing
   that will engulf your dreams.
   There is no land for you to return,
   no land to inherit.

(continued)

---

[17] A lyric from "When You and I Were Young, Maggie," an American folk song
introduced by missionaries to Korea around 1856, then adapted and translated by Ki
In-sik, retitled "Megiui Chu-eok [Memory of Maggie]."

(여의도 광시곡)

6

지렁이들도 꾸물꾸물 꿈을 꾸기 시작하고
네온사인의 젖은 미소 피어오르고
地下의 死者들도 감겼던 눈을
일제히 치켜뜨고 地上을 응시하는,
거두절미하고, 밤이 온다.
반신불수의 밤, 그러나 영혼불멸의 밤.
반짝이는 눈을 가진 쥐새끼들은
포식의 탁자 위에서 공영방송과
분냄새 나는 잡지들과 주식회사
경영 방침을 논의하며
한 사회의 아마도 광대한 몇 바퀴의 헛바퀴와
한 개인의 아마도 무수한 개미 쳇바퀴가
여전히 맞물려 돌아가면서
잘 구도된, 또 하나의 완벽한
폐허를 향해 전진해가고,

여의도는 뒤로 벌렁 누운
거대한 다족류의 벌레.
그 무수한 발끝마다 네온사인을 달고
허공을 향해 수만 개의 발가락을 꼬물거리면서
입으로는 하루종일 먹었던 온갖 더러움을
게거품처럼 조용히 게워내고

여의도 허공 가장 깊숙한 곳에선
神의 형상을 한 거대한 검은 아가리가
이 세계의 남은 뼈를 아득아득 씹고 있다.

—여의도는 거룩한
天上의 빵.

기억의 집

(*Yeoui Island Rhapsody*)

6

Even earthworms start to wriggle and dream,
even the damp smiles of neon signs bloom,
even the dead underground simultaneously
open their eyes and gaze at the ground above—
long story short, here comes the night:
the half-paralyzed night, yet the night everlasting.
On gluttony's table baby rats with glimmering eyes
discuss public broadcasting,
and perfume-scented magazines
and corporate management policies.
The wheels of society perhaps immense yet few and futile,
the merry-go-rounds of individuals perhaps numerous
　　　yet ant-tiny,
all spin in gear as always
and march towards the one more
well designed perfect ruin.

Yeoui Island is a giant millipede
flipped on its back.
Dangling neon signs from each of its myriad feet,
wriggling tens of thousands of toes towards the empty air,
vomiting all the filth devoured throughout the day
quietly like crab-froth from its mouth.

In the deepest spot of Yeoui Island's empty air
one giant black mouth in God's image
crunches and munches the leftover bones of this world.
　　　　　　　　　—Yeoui Island is the holy
　　　　　　　　　bread of heaven.

告白

토해놓은 내장을 이젠 도로 삼키겠어요.
제자리에 다 삼키고서
이쁜 플라스틱 살로 가리겠어요.

이마와 양 뺨엔 박제된 눈물방울들을
구슬 장식처럼 은은히 달고서,
두 눈 감고 뿌리부터
몰래몰래 썩기 시작하겠어요.

죽을 때까지 당신들을 교묘히 속이겠어요.
당신들이 안녕히 속을 수 있기만을 바랄 뿐예요.

속이고 또 속일 수 없는 어느 순간
거짓말처럼 가비얍게
내 일평생을 건너뛰어 버리겠어요.

(어쩌면 나의 외알 안경이
실수로 한 번쯤 눈물을 흘릴지도 모르지만.)

CONFESSION

The guts I threw up I will now swallow back.
I will swallow all back into their places
and veil them with pretty plastic flesh.

Adorn my cheeks and forehead
with taxidermied teardrops misty as bead pendants,
close my eyes and from my root
I will secretly quietly begin to rot.

Till my dying day I will cunningly deceive you all.
I only wish you to be safely deceived.

At the moment when I can no longer deceive you
light as a lie
I will leap over my lifetime.

(Although possibly by mistake
my monocle might just tear up once or twice.)

Y를 위하여

너는 날 버렸지,
이젠 헤어지자고
너는 날 버렸지,
산속에서 바닷가에서
나는 날 버렸지.

수술대 위에 다리를 벌리고 누웠을 때
시멘트 지붕을 뚫고 하늘이 보이고
날아가는 새들의 폐벽에 가득 찬 공기도 보였어.

하나 둘 셋 넷 다섯도 못 넘기고
지붕도 하늘도 새도 보이잖고
그러나 난 죽으면서 보았어.
나와 내 아이가 이 도시의 시궁창 속으로 시궁창 속으로
세월의 자궁 속으로 한없이 흘러가던 것을.
그때부터야.
나는 이 지상에 한 무덤으로 누워 하늘을 바라고
나의 아이는 하늘을 날아다닌다.
올챙이꼬리 같은 지느러미를 달고.
　나쁜 놈, 난 널 죽여버리고 말 거야
　널 내 속에서 다시 낳고야 말 거야
내 아이는 드센 바람에 불려 지상에 떨어지면
내 무덤 속에서 몇 달 간 따스하게 지내다
또다시 떠나가지 저 차가운 하늘 바다로,
올챙이꼬리 같은 지느러미를 달고.
오 개새끼
못 잊어!

　　　　　　　　　　　　기억의 집

⬚⬚■ ‖ ■⬚⬚

FOR Y

You abandoned me,
saying time to break up now,
you abandoned me,
on the mountain at the seashore
I abandoned myself.

Lying on the operating table as I spread my legs
I saw the sky through the cement roof,
I saw the air filling the lungs of flying birds.

One two three four couldn't even count five
no roof no sky no bird no more,
but while dying I saw
my child and me flowing into this city's sewer,
    into the sewer
flowing endlessly into the womb of time.
It is since then.
Lying on this earth as a tomb I gaze up at the sky
and in that sky my child flies.
Wearing a fin like a tadpole tail.
    Dirty bastard, I'll kill you in the end
    In the end I'll give birth to you inside me again
Blown by rough winds, if plunged to earth
my child tarries warm in my tomb for a few months
then departs again to that cold sea sky,
wearing a fin like a tadpole tail.
Oh son of a bitch
I cannot forget!

20년 후에, 芝에게

지금 네 눈빛이 닿으면 유리창은 숨을 쉰다.
지금 네가 그린 파란 물고기는 하늘 물 속에서 뛰놀고
풀밭에선 네 작은 종아리가 바람에 날아다니고,

이상하지,
살아 있다는 건,
참 아슬아슬하게 아름다운 일이란다.
빈 벌판에서 차갑고도 따스한 비를 맞고 있는 것 같지.
눈만 뜨면 신기로운 것들이
네 눈의 수정체 속으로 헤엄쳐 들어오고
때로 너는 두 팔 벌려, 환한 빗물을 받으며 미소짓고……
이윽고 어느 날 너는 새로운 눈(眼)을 달고
세상으로 출근하리라.

많은 사람들을 너는 만날 것이고
많은 사람들이 네 눈물의 외줄기 길을 타고 떠나가리라.
강물은 흘러가 다시 돌아오지 않고
너는 네 스스로 江을 이뤄 흘러가야만 한다.

그러나 나의 몫은 이제 깊이깊이 가라앉는 일. 봐라,
저 많은 세월의 개떼들이 나를 향해 몰려 오잖니,
흰 이빨과 흰 꼬리를 치켜들고
푸른 파도를 타고 달려오잖니.
물려죽지 않기 위해, 하지만 끝내 물려죽으면서,
나는 깊이깊이 추락해야 해.
발바닥부터 서서히 꺼져들어가며, 참으로
연극적으로 죽어가는 게 실은 나의 사랑인 까닭에.

(계속)

기억의 집

20 YEARS LATER, TO JIE

Now, now the windowpane breathes as your eyes fall upon it.
Now, the blue fish you drew romps in the watery sky
and your tiny calves flutter in the wind over the grass.

How strange,
to be alive,
what a perilously beautiful thing it is.
As if standing in an open field under chill but warming rain.
Whenever you open your eyes
wondrous things swim into your crystalline lens,
sometimes you open your arms, smile under
      radiant rainwater ...
Someday before long you will get fresh vision
and leave home to work in the world.

You will meet many people,
but many people will leave you treading on your lone
      trail of tears.
The river flows and never returns,
you must form a river and flow for yourself.

Now my role is to submerge deeply. Look,
look at the packdogs of time storming towards me.
Look at them speeding towards me riding on blue waves,
brandishing their white teeth and tails.
Not to be bitten to death, yet dying from their bites after all,
I must plunge deeply.
Extinguishing gradually up from my soles, for truly,
dying theatrically is my love indeed.

(continued)

□□□ ‖ □□□

(20년 후에, 芝에게)

그리하여 21세기의 어느 하오,
거리에 비 내리듯
내 무덤에 술 내리고
나는 알지

어느 알지 못할 꿈의 어귀에서
잠시 울고 서 있을 네 모습을,
이윽고 네가 찾아 헤맬 모든 길들을,
―가다가 아름답고 슬픈 사람들을 만나면
그들의 동냥바가지에 너의 소중한 은화 한 닢도
기쁘게 던져주며
마침내 네가 이르게 될 모든 끝의

시작을!

기억의 집

□□□ ‖ □□□

(20 Years Later, To Jie)

Therefore in some twenty-first century afternoon,
when alcohol showers my tomb
like rain showers the streets,
I will see

your silhouette that will stand a while in tears
at some obscure dream entrance,
and all the roads you will wander in quest by and by,
and that of all the ends you will finally reach
—after casting gladly
even your last precious silver coin into the bowls
of beautiful sorrowful people on your way

the beginning!

無題 1

1

나는 그들을 살아넘겼다.
그러므로 나는 이미 내가 아니다.
이제 죽어도, 죽어서도
더 나아갈 곳은 없고

나는 이제 노래하라!
입도 혓바닥도 없이,

처음으로 마음이 찢어지고
마지막으로 항문이 찢어질 때까지
나는 이제 영원히 춤추라!
무릎도 발바닥도 없이,

노예선의 북소리 울리고
까마귀들의 습격이 시작될 때까지.

(계속)

□□■ ‖ ■□□

UNTITLED 1

1

I outlived them.
Therefore I am no longer myself.
Even if I die now, even after my death
nowhere further to proceed—

So I, sing now!
With no mouth no tongue,

till my heart rips at first
till my anus rips at last
now I, dance forever!
With no knees no soles,

till the drums rumble from the slave ship
till the crows launch their surprise attack.

(continued)

(無題 1)

2

구르기로 작정하면 한없이 굴러지지만,
그러나 육체는 흘러가도
마음은 흘러가지 못하며,

어머님.
저 바다 끝 너머
내 망막의 수평선에 누워 계신
종이 같은, 뿌리 없는 어머님,
가여운 내⋯⋯

내 너를 무릎 위에 얹고
가리라 가리라
앉은뱅이 시늉으로
내 너를 무덤까지 데려가리라
무덤 속에 최초로 씨 뿌리리라

(어디에도 계시옵지 않은
그대, 독기로 타오르시며
그대, 한 세상을 꺾어버리시며
그대, 그대 그늘로 일세를 뒤덮으시며,
그러나 원하신다면,
당신이 원하는 그 깊이로
고이 추락하리라.)

(계속)

(Untitled 1)

2

Once decided I can roll forever,
but even if my body can
my mind cannot flow on.

Mother.
Lying on my retina's horizon
beyond that sea's end,
papery, rootless mother,
my poor ...

Placing you on my lap
I will go I will go.
Mimicking a cripple
I will carry you to the tomb.
I will sow in the tomb for the first time.

(Existing nowhere,
dear, burning with spite
dear, breaking a world
dear, casting your shadow over an age—
but if you wish,
into the depth of your wish
I will peacefully fall.)

(continued)

(無題 1)

3

머나먼 소혹성 위에서
그녀가 까마득하게 외쳐댄다.
우리가 그녀의 외침을 듣지 못하는 것은,
우리가 듣고 싶어하지 않는 귀를 가진 까닭이다.
그러나 내 무의식의 코는 분명하게 찾아낸다.
이 파멸의 냄새,
보이잖게 살이 타는 푸른 냄새를.

책이 썩고
애인이 썩고
한 나라가 썩고

아랫목에서 어머니가 썩고 계시다.

4

보이네
한밤중에
그대의 흰 죽음.

모든 事物이 까무러치고
모든 事物의 表象이 까무러치고

보이네
한밤중에
떠가는 그대의 흰 죽음.

(계속)

기억의 집

□·□ ‖ ■·■

(Untitled 1)

3

From a minor planet far away
she goes on faintly shouting.
The reason we cannot hear her
is because we have ears unwilling to listen.
But the nose of my unconscious keenly finds it,
this scent of wreck,
this blue scent of invisibly scorching flesh.

A book rots
a lover rots
a country rots

and a mother rots on a warm floor.

4

I see
at midnight
your white death.

All objects swoon,
all objects' symbols swoon,

I see
at midnight
your white death floating away.

(continued)

(無題 1)

5

　　—그러나 언어는 여전히 하나의 울타리일 뿐이며,
　　'인간은 결국 자기 자신만을 체험할 뿐이다.'

기다려라, 이제 보다 아픈 가을이 오고
비로소 나는 그치지 않는 잠을 자기 시작하리라.
두문불출 내 마음의 세월 위에
그대들의 물음이 떨어져내리고
떨어져내려도
답하지 않으리라,
어느 날 문득 내 창가에 불이 꺼질 때까지.

⬛ ‖ ⬛

(Untitled 1)

5

But to the end language remains a mere enclosure
and "in the end humans experience nothing but themselves."

Wait, a more painful autumn is yet to come
and finally I'll begin to sleep the unending sleep.
Even if your questions cascade
and cascade
over my mind's secluded days,
I will not answer,
till some day suddenly my window light goes out.

無題 2

1

간밤 소리 없이 이슬 내린 뒤
현관문이 가만히 울고
죽음은 우유 배달부의 길을 타고 온다.

누군가의 검은 눈빛,
늘어진 검은 손이
문고리를 부여잡고

순간, 거대한 그림자가
타이탄 트럭처럼 나를 덮치고
들렸다,
캄캄하게 낙락장송 쓰러지는 소리,
캄캄하게 한 시대가 길게 뻗는 소리.

(계속)

UNTITLED 2

1

After mist fell silently overnight
the front door cries softly
and death approaches along the milkman's path.

Someone's dark glance
limp black hand
clutched the doorknob

and suddenly, a giant shadow
fell on me like a Mack truck[18]
and I heard
the sound of a tall thriving pine dismally falling,
the sound of an age dismally stretching.

(continued)

---

[18] Choi refers to the "Titan," a large four-wheel Korean truck developed by Kia in 1971. Since the size of the truck is what is remarkable in the poem, I translated this as the "Mack" tractor-trailer truck, which is among the largest vehicles on the road in North America.

(無題 2)

2

1983년, 운명의 맞물림이 풀어지는 소리,
무한 궤도 속으로 떨어져 나가는 작은 객차 하나,
1983년, 하나님은 경솔했고
나는 부실했다.

오 이 모든 진땀나는 공포! 공포!
이 세계를, 이 세계의 맨살의 공포를
나는 감당할 수 없다.
그러나 밀려온다,
이 세계는,
내 눈알의 깊은 망막을 향해
수십 억의 군화처럼 행군해온다.

눈감아요, 이제 곧 무서운 시간이 와요.
창자나 골수 같은 건 모두 쏟아버려요.
토해버려요, 한 시대의 썩은 음식물들을,
현실의 잠, 잠의 현실 속에서.
그리고 깊이깊이 가라앉아요.

(고요히 한 세월의 밑바닥을 기어가며
나는 다족류의 벌레로 변해갔다.)

(계속)

기억의 집

◨ ‖ ◨

(Untitled 2)

2

In 1983, the sound of fate unfastening its grip,
a small passenger train falling onto an infinite track.
In 1983, God was flippant
and I was feeble.

Oh all this sweaty fear! Fear!
I cannot bear
this world, the naked fear of this world.
But this world,
presses on,
towards the deep retinas of my eyes,
marches in like millions of combat boots.

Close your eyes, the dreadful time is yet to come.
In the sleep of reality, in the reality of sleep,
throw everything out, like guts or marrow,
throw up the rotten food of an age,
now sink deeply down.

(Crawling quietly at the bottom of time
I turned into a millipede.)

(continued)

(無題 2)

3

이 시대 죽음의 잔은
이미 채워졌으니
네 몫은 필요치 않다.
그러니 가라!
어서 되돌아가라!

(한밤중에 문득 잠에서 깨어날 때
너희의 거울 속을 들여다보라.
거기, 이십세기의 치욕인 내가
너희에게 은은한 치욕의 미소를 보내고 있을 것이다.)

만장하신 여러분
나를 죽이고 싶어 환장하신 여러분
오늘 내가 죽는 쇼는 이것으로 끝입니다.
십 년 후 똑같은 시각에
똑같은 염통을 달고
이 장소로 나와주십시오.

(계속)

기억의 집

□□□ ‖ □□□

(Untitled 2)

3

THIS AGE'S CUP OF DEATH
IS ALREADY FULL,
YOUR PORTION IS NOT NEEDED.
THEREFORE GO BACK!
LEAVE AT ONCE!

(If you suddenly awake at midnight
look into your mirrors.
I, the shame of the twentieth century, will
be there sending you an elusive smile of shame.)

Ladies and gentlemen
who lost your minds itching to kill me,
this is the last episode of the "My Death Today."
At the exact time ten years from now
please come out here again
bearing your exact same hearts.

(continued)

(無題 2)

4

가을이 첫 국화송이를 맺을 때
어머니 한평생 미뤄오던
한숨 피워올리시고
표표히, 표표히 흩어지는 달무리.
살아 있는 자들은 그래도 하루의 양식을 즐길 것이며
살아 행복한 자들은 두 번째 아이를 만들리니
설명할 수 없어 이 세계는 눕고
설명할 수 없어 이 세계의 길은 허공에 뜨고

한 체험의 파도의 깊이를 타고
한 채의 집이 금이 가
달빛만 받아도 기우뚱거리고,
들리누나, 오밤중에 웬 거인이
온 세상에 교교하게 오줌 누는 소리.

("담 밖에서 나를 엿보는 자 있으니
필시 나의 다른 마음일지라.")

(계속)

기억의 집

(Untitled 2)

4

When autumn bears the first chrysanthemum bud
my mother exhales the sigh
kept inside her whole life—
the softly, softly diffusing halo of the moon.
The living will nonetheless enjoy the day's bread,
the happily living will indeed make their second child—
being inexplicable, this world lies down,
being inexplicable, this world's path rises in
    the empty air.

Riding the wave-depth of an experience
a house cracks and falters
even at a touch of moonlight,
and I hear at midnight the sound of a giant
pissing luminously on the whole world.

("Someone is spying on me behind the wall
and it must be my other mind.")

(continued)

(無題 2)

5

어머니는 걸어가신다, 내 머릿속에서.
세상 한 켠을 고즈너기 울리며
어머니는 걸어가신다, 자꾸만 지구 반대편으로.
오래 걷고 오래 수고하며

해왕성을 지나 명왕성을 지나
쉬임 없이 내 꿈속을 걸어
마침내 어느 아침, 어머니는
내 문간에 당도하시리라.

그리고 이제 빛나지 않는 나날의 무덤 속에서
그러나 가능한 한 빛을 향해
한 아이가 태어날 준비를 서두르고 있다,
未明의 회색 창가에서.

문 밖에선 새벽 산길을 돌아온
그와 그의 마차가 나를 기다리고

멀리, 갇힌 수평선의 벽을 깨뜨리며
피묻은 갈매기 한 마리가 탈출한다.

기억의 집

⊡■■ ‖ ■■⊡

(Untitled 2)

5

My mother walks away, in my head.
Resonating gently on one side of the world
my mother walks away, repeatedly, across the earth.
Walking for a long time, toiling for a long time,

passing Neptune, passing Pluto,
walking restlessly in my dream,
finally one morning, my mother
will arrive at my doorstep.

And now in the tomb of no-longer-lit days
yet toward the only light possible,
a child hastily prepares its own birth
by the gray window of early dawn.

Outside the door he and his carriage await me
back from the mountain drive at dawn.

And far away, breaking through the locked horizon
one bloody seagull escapes.

문명

어느 날 한 사람이 블랙 홀로 빨려들어간다.
어느 날 두 사람이 블랙 홀로 빨려들어간다.
어느 날 네 사람이 블랙 홀로 빨려들어간다.
어느 날 사만 명이 블랙 홀로 빨려들어간다.
어느 날 …… 어느 날……
어느 날 지구는 잠잠 무사하고

텅 빈 아시아 대륙
황량한 사막 위로 모래바람이 불어가고
마지막으로, 실패한 한 남자 곁에
한사코, 실패한 한 여자가 눕는다.
어디선가 붉은 양수가 질펀하게
새어 흐르기 시작하고

(누구, 너희는 누구?)
허공 한 구석에서
외계인의 눈알 하나가
조소처럼 빛나고 있다.

□■■ || ■■□

CIVILIZATION

One day one person gets sucked into a black hole.
One day two people get sucked into a black hole.
One day four people get sucked into a black hole.
One day forty thousand people get sucked into
      a black hole.
One day ... One day ...
One day the earth gets peaceful and quiet.

Over the empty Asian continent
over its barren desert the sand storm blows,
and for the last time, next to a failed man,
desperately, a failed woman lies down.
Oozing amply from somewhere,
red amniotic fluid begins to flow.

(Who, who are you people?)
at a corner of empty air
one eyeball of an alien
shines like a sneer.

슬로 비디오

한 사람이
죽어가고 있다.
어두운 화면
흐린 일생 위에서.

이 패주의 길
오냐 다시 오마
이빨을 갈며

그러나 한 사람이
죽어가고 있다.

그는 분명 쓰러질 것이다.
고통처럼 행복처럼
기필코 그는 쓰러질 것이다.
사람이 쓰러지면
어떻게 쓰러지는가를
당신들에게 보여주기 위해서,
슬로 슬로 비디오로,
겨드랑이 털의 미세한 떨림까지.

그는 당신들의 필생의 악몽이 되고자 한다.

피하고 싶은 자는
그것을 복수심이라 일컬으며
채널을 돌려버리면 된다.
그리고 밥상머리에서 입 안에 든
밥알을 오래오래 씹고 있거라.

기억의 집

·■■ ‖ ■■·

SLOW-MOTION VIDEO

A man
is dying.
On the dark screen
of an obscure lifetime.

Sure I'll come again
to this road of defeat
—gritting his teeth

Yet, a man
is dying.

Surely he will fall.
Like pain like happiness
certainly he will fall.
To show you
how a man falls
when a man falls,
with slow slow-motion video,
down to the minute quivers of his armpit hair.

He wills to be the nightmare of your lifetime.

Whoever wants to avoid it
can call it vengeance
and change the channel.
Then at the head of the dinner table
chew the morsel in your mouth for a long time.

放

가을날 사과 떨어지듯
아는 얼굴 하나 땅속에 묻히고
세월이 잘 가느냐 못 잘 가느냐
두 바지가랑이가 싸우며 낡아가고

어이어이 거기 계신 이 누구신가,
평생토록 내 문 밖에서
날 기다리시는 이 누구신가?

이제 그대가 내 적이 아님을 알았으니,
언제든 그대 원할 때 들어오라.

134

□□□ ‖ □□□

RELEASE

Like an apple on an autumn day
one familiar face fell and buried in the ground,
and inseams wear out bickering
whether the times go well or not.

Hey-hey, who are you over there,
who are you outside the door
waiting for me my whole life?

Now that I know you are not my enemy,
you may come in whenever you wish.

자칭 詩

그러면 다시 말해볼까.
삶에 관하여, 삶의 풍경에 관하여,
주리를 틀 시대에 관하여.
아니 아니, 잘못하면 자칭 詩가 쏟아질 것 같아
나는 모든 틈을 잠그고
나 자신을 잠근다.
(詩여 모가지여,
가늘고도 모진 詩의 모가지여)
그러나 비틀어 잠가도, 새어나온다.
썩은 물처럼,
송장이 썩어나오는 물처럼.

내 삶의 썩은 즙,
한잔 드시겠습니까?
(극소량의 詩를 토해내고 싶어하는
귀신이 내 속에서 살고 있다.)

□□■ ‖ ■□□

WANNABE POETRY

If so, shall I try to talk again?
About life, about the landscape of life,
about the age deserving thumb-screw torture.
No no, if not careful wannabe poetry might spurt out,
so I zip all the cracks,
so I zip myself.
(Oh poetry, oh the neck,
thin but tenacious, oh the neck of poetry)
Yet however I twist and zip, it leaks.
Like rotten water,
like water oozing from a rotten corpse.

Rotten juice of my life,
would you like a cup?
(A ghost lives inside me who wants
to vomit the poetic minimum.)

돌아와 나는 詩를 쓰고

고통의 잔치는 이제 끝났다.
기억의 되새김만이 남았을 뿐.

그러나 장르를 바꾸고
운명의 제목을 바꾸고
그러고도 살아남은 고통의 기억들.
그 위로 안개처럼 내리는 잠의 實重量.

슬프다 가이없다
돌아와 나는 詩를 쓰고
한 세기가 흘러가고
돌아와 나는 또 詩를 쓰고.

여기는 어디인가,
내 일생의 유적지인가,
전생인가, 내세인가.

흔들며 흔들리며
눈뜬 잠의 나날을
나는 잠행하고

내가 몸 눕히는 곳 어디서나
슬픔은 반짝인다.
하늘의 별처럼
地上의 똥처럼

▫▪◼ ‖ ◼▪▫

RETURN, I WRITE POETRY

It's over now, the party of pain.
The rumination of memories is all that's left.

Yet after changing the genre,
changing the fate's title,
surviving still, memories of pain.
Misting over them, the true weight of sleep.

How sad, how endless—
return, I write poetry,
one century passes away,
return, I again write poetry.

Where is this,
the ruins of my life,
a previous life, an afterlife?

Swaying and swayed
I travel in disguise
through days of open-eyed sleep

and wherever I lay my body
sadness gleams
like stars in the sky
like shit on the earth.

봄의 略史

서울신문사와 시청이 두 개의 사이드를
이루는 일방통로를 걸어, 걸어!
XX協會, 그 미궁의 문을 향해
몸을 꺽고 정신을 꺽을 때,
유물론은 내 머릿속에서
가장 확실하게 빛난다.
유물론은 나의 슬픔,
유물론은 나의 오기.

기워도 기워도 나의 삶은
자꾸만 펑크가 터지고
(분명 어딘가 구조적 모순이 있다)

내가 버린 세월, 내가 포기한 세월 위에
올해도 수백 펜지꽃들 피어난다.

지랄처럼, 간질 발작처럼
펜지꽃들 미칠미칠 피어나
텅 빈 봄의 전면을 뒤덮고,
오 가벼운 약속의 시간들이여
흐르는 잠과 하품과 구역질의 시간들이여.

만월처럼 現世의 毒이 차오르누나.

□·□ ‖ ■·■

BRIEF HISTORY OF SPRING

Walk! Walk along that one-way street
between the Seoul Newspaper and City Hall.
When I bend my body, bend my spirit
toward that labyrinthine door of XX Society,
materialism shines
most certainly in my head.
Materialism, my sadness,
materialism, my pride.

Though I patch and patch again
my life gets punctured again and again
(surely there's a structural contradiction somewhere)

and again this year hundreds of pansies bloom
over the times I abandoned, over the times I gave up.

Like going nuts, like having fits
madly frantically pansies erupt
and cover the entire face of empty spring—
oh the hours of frivolous promises,
oh the hours of flowing sleep, yawns and nausea.

Like a full moon there waxes the poison of
        the present age.

물망초

우리가 엽전 열닷 냥 찌개 백반의
자유를 위해 분주할 때에도

모든 길들은 소리 없이 굽이치며 않고,
보이지 않는 곳에서 물망초들은 피어난다.

외부를 향한 내부의 내부의
피흘림을 고요히 지우며
물망초는 또 한 가지를 뻗는다.

그와 같이 내 낮은 흐느낌 또한
하나의 말이 될 수 있을 때까지

잠시만 기다려다오.

내가 이 잔을 다 비울 때까지
내가 꿈속에서 다시 한 번만 돌아누울 때까지
내가 내 시야를 스스로 거둘 때까지

잠시만 기다려다오,

죽음이여
잠시만,
영원히.

기억의 집

□□■ ‖ ■□□

A FORGET-ME-NOT

Even when we bustle for the freedom
of a meal worth fifteen coins

heaving silently all roads ache,
somewhere invisible forget-me-nots bloom.

Erasing quietly the bleeding
of its interior's interior towards its exterior,
a forget-me-not stretches forth yet another branch.

Till my low sobbing too
can become an utterance like that

please wait a moment.

Till I empty this cup completely
till I toss in my dream one last time
till I roll up my field of vision myself.

Please wait a moment,

dear death,
just a moment,
forever.

서녘 항구

저무는 해 닻을 내리고

서녘 항구,
불타는 관절염의 뼈들을 이끌고
나 여기까지 왔네.

흔들어, 흔들어줘!
순교도 배교도 구원이 될 수 없는 시대,
침묵하는 배들이 바닷속에 뿌리내릴 때
내 일생을 내 일평생을
흔들어, 흔들어줘!

기억의 집

WESTERN HARBOR

The setting sun lowers its anchor

to the Western Harbor,
dragging my bones burning with arthritis
I came this far.

Shake, give it a shake!
In an age when no martyrdom, no apostasy can be
    a redemption,
when silent ships root down into the sea,
my life, my whole life,
shake, give it a shake!

기억의 집

그 많은 좌측과 우측을 돌아
나는 약속의 땅에
다다르지 못했다.

도처에서 물과 바람이 새는
허공의 房에 누워, "내게 다오,
그 증오의 손길을, 복수의 꽃잎을"
노래하던 그 여자도 오래 전에
재가 되어 부스러져내렸다.

그리하여, 이것은 무엇인가.
내 운명인가, 나의 꿈인가,
운명이란 스스로 꾸는 꿈의 다른 이름인가.

기억의 집에는 늘 불안한 바람이 삐걱이고
기억의 집에는 늘 불요불급한
슬픔의 세간살이들이 넘치고,

살아 있음의 내 나날 위에 무엇을 쓸 것인가.
무엇을 더 보태고 무엇을 더 빼야 할 것인가.

자세히 보면 고요히 흔들리는 벽,
더 자세히 보면 고요히 갈라지는 벽,
그 속에서 소리 없이 살고 있는 이들의 그림자,
혹은 긴 한숨 소리.

(계속)

⬜◻◼ ‖ ◼◻⬜

HOUSE OF MEMORY

So many turns to the right and the left
I could not reach
the promised land.

Lying in the room in the empty air
where wind and water seep in every crevice,
the woman who used to sing "Give me
those hands of hatred, petals of revenge"
turned to ash too and crumbled long ago.

Then, what is this?
Is this my fate, is this my dream,
is fate another name for a self-dreaming dream?

In the house of memory an uneasy wind always creaks,
in the house of memory nonessential sundries
of sadness always overflow—

What more should I write across my living days?
What more should I add, what more should I subtract?

If I look close it's a quietly shaking wall,
if I look closer it's a quietly cracking wall—
the shadows of people silently living inside,
or the sound of their long sighs.

(continued)

(기억의 집)

무엇을 더 보태고 무엇을 더 빼야 할 것인가.
일찍이 나 그들 중의 하나였으며
지금도 하나이지만,
잠시 눈감으면 다시 닫히는 벽,
다시 갇히는 사람들.
갇히는 것은 나이지만,
벽의 안쪽도 벽, 벽의 바깥도 벽이지만.

내가 바라보는 이 세계
벽이 꾸는 꿈.

저무는 어디선가
굶주린 그리운 눈동자들이 피어나고
한평생의 꿈이 먼 별처럼
결빙해가는 창가에서

나는 다시 한 번

아버지의 나라
그 물빛 흔들리는 강가에 다다르고 싶다.

⊡⊡■ ‖ ■⊡⊡

(House of Memory)

What more should I add, what more should I subtract?
Before, I was one of them
and though one of them still,
if I blink for a second, the again-closing wall,
the again-confined people.
Though it's me who is confined,
though it's a wall inside of, outside of the wall.

This world I gaze at,
the dream the wall dreams.

Darkening somewhere
hungry yearning eyes kindle,
and from the windowside where
my lifelong-dream freezes like a star far away

I once again

ache to reach the fatherland,
that wavering, watergreen riverside.

이제 가야만 한다

때로 낭만주의적 지진아의 고백은
눈물겹기도 하지만,
이제 가야만 한다.
몹쓸 고통은 버려야만 한다.

한때 한없는 고통의 가속도,
가속도의 취기에 실려
나 폭풍처럼
세상 끝을 헤매었지만
그러나 고통이라는 말을
이제 결코 발음하고 싶지 않다.

파악할 수 없는 이 세계 위에서
나는 너무 오래 뒤뚱거리고만 있었다.

목구멍과 숨을 위해서는
動詞만으로 충분하고,
내 몸보다 그림자가 먼저 허덕일지라도
오냐 온몸 온정신으로
이 세상을 관통해보자

내가 더 이상 나를 죽일 수 없을 때
내가 더 이상 나를 죽일 수 없는 곳에서
혹 내가 피어나리라.

·■□ ‖ ■□·

NOW THEY MUST GO

Though confessions of a romantic retard
can be touching at times,
now they must go.
Malignant pains must be discarded.

Once, carried by the infinite acceleration of pain,
by the drunkenness of that acceleration,
like a storm I
roamed the world's end,
but now I prefer never
to utter the word pain.

On this ungraspable earth for too long
I have done nothing but falter.

Verbs alone will suffice
for my throat and breath,
even if my shadow gasps before my body,
yes, let me penetrate this world
with my body and spirit.

When I can no longer kill myself
where I can no longer kill myself
perhaps I might revive.

희망의 감옥

1

내 희망이 문을 닫는 시각에
너는 기어코 두드린다.
나의 것보다 더욱 캄캄한 희망 혹은 절망으로.

벽도 내부도 없이
문만으로 서로 닫혀진
이 열린 희망의 감옥.

네 절망이 문을 닫는 시각에
나는 기어코 두드린다.
너의 것보다 더욱 캄캄한 절망 혹은 희망으로.

2

그대, 헤매는 그림자
내 발목에 묶어맬 수 없으니,
그대 긴 악몽의 밤을, 잠을,
내 깨어 있음으로 보완할 수 없으니,
형이여, 사랑하는 형제여
부디 그대의 악몽을 딛고서
그대 본래의 빛으로 빛나라.

(계속)

PRISON OF HOPE

1

At the closing time of my hope
you knock at last.
With hope or despair much darker than mine.

With no wall, no interior,
closed from each other only by a door,
this open prison of hope.

At the closing time of your despair
I knock at last.
With despair or hope much darker than yours.

2

Dear, since I cannot tie
your wandering shadow to my ankle,
since I cannot aid with my vigil
your long nightmarish night, your sleep,
brother, my beloved sibling,
may you surmount your nightmare
and shine with your original light.

(continued)

(희망의 감옥)

3

어떻게 하라고 깊고 깊은
오리무중의 밤은 말하지 않는다.
밤은 단지 애매하게 손가락을 쳐들어 보일 뿐이다.
그곳을 향해 나는 먼저
의문을 찾아나서야 하고
그리고 대답을 찾아나서야 한다.
대답에 이르기 전의
의문의 사냥꾼이 가야 할 길은
얼마나 머나먼가.

4

흰 새털구름이 떠 있는 동안은
그대의 이웃은 그대의 이웃.
그러나 먹구름이 몰려오기 시작하면
벌판엔 그대 혼자뿐
그리워 그리워
그대가 그 문을 두드리되
그 문은 언제나 닫혀 있더이다.

5

저 혼자 자유로워서는
새가 되지 못한다.
새가 되기 위해서는
새를 동경하는
수많은 다른 눈(眼)들이 있어야만 한다.

(계속)

기억의 집

·□■ ‖ ■□·

(Prison of Hope)

3

How to do it the deep dark
enigmatic night does not say.
The night only points its finger ambiguously.
To get there I must
first set out for a question,
then set out for an answer.
How long the path is
a question-hunter must tread
to get to an answer.

4

As long as white feather-clouds float,
your neighbors are your neighbors.
But as soon as black storm-clouds flock,
you are all alone in the field.
Yearn and yearn
though you pound on the door,
that door always remains closed.

5

By being free alone
one cannot become a bird.
To become a bird
there must be numerous other eyes
admiring the bird.

(continued)

□□□ ‖ □□□

(희망의 감옥)

6

풍경을 닫아라,
오늘은 祭日.
이 세상은 관광지가 아니며
너의 방은 스쳐지나가는
열차의 창문이 아니다.
마지막으로, 숨을 닫아라,
오늘은 亡日.
(주여, 때가 가까웠나이다.
제발 이때를 놓치지 마소서.
아니 제발 이때를 놓쳐주소서.)

7

비 온다,
비 간다.
사람 사는 골목 어디서나
흙 젖고 창틀 젖고
다시 마른다.
현재 미래 혹은 내세를 위해
어느 집에나 대문 있다.
어느 방에나 창문 있다.
…………
…………
말하기 싫다.
말하기 싫다는
말을 나는 말한다.

(희망은 감옥이다.)

‣▪◾ ‖ ◾▪‣

(Prison of Hope)

6

Shut down the scenery,
it's memorial day today.
This world is not a sight
nor your room a window
on a passing train.
Lastly, shut down your breath,
it's ruination day today.
(Jesus, the time is near.
Please do not miss this moment.
No, please do miss this moment.)

7

Rain comes,
rain goes.
Along any alley people live
the soil, the window frames
dampen again and dry again.
For the present or the future or the afterlife,
there's a gate before any house,
there are windows in any room.
...
...
I don't like to talk.
I talk the talk that
I don't like to talk.

(Hope is the prison.)

□□□ ‖ □□□

돌아와 이제

새들은 항시 낮게 낮게 가라앉고
산발한 그리움은 밖에서,
밖에서만 날 부르고

쉬임 없는 파문과 파문 사이에서
나는 너무 오랫동안 춤추었다.

이젠 너를 떠나야 하리.

어화 어화 우리 슬픔
여기까지 노저어 왔었나.

내 너를 큰물 가운데 두고
이제 차마 떠나야 하리.

오래 전에 내 눈 속 깊이 가라앉았던 별,
다시 떠오르는 별.
오래 갈구해온 나의 땅에
다시 피가 돌고
돌아와 이제 내 울타리를 고치느니,

허술함이여 허술함이여
버려진 잡초들이
이미 내 키를 넘었구나

RETURN, NOW

Birds always sank down and down
and disheveled yearning called me
from outside, only from outside—

between these restless ripples
I have danced for too long.

I must leave you now.

Oh dear Oh dear, when did
our sorrow row us this far?

Leaving you amidst this deluge
now I must bring myself to leave.

The star sunken long ago deep into my eyes,
the star rises again.
Through my long-desired land
blood circulates again,
and return, now I mend my fences.

Oh dilapidation dilapidation
abandoned weeds
already grew over my head.

주변인의 초상

이 세계의 문법을 그는 매번 배우지만
매번 잊어버린다.
세계가 마취된 것인가,
자신의 두개골이 마취된 것인가,
그는 매번 판정을 내리지 못한다.
그는 물질이 정신성으로, 정신이 물질성으로
이동해가는 통로를 너무나 잘 알고
때로는 너무나 까마득히 모른다.

주변인은 신문이 배달되는 시각과
텔레비전이 시작되는 시각을
습관적으로 초조히 기다린다.
주변인은 이따금씩 제 집안의
하나뿐인 시계가 맞는지 알아보기 위해
국번 없이 116에 전화를 걸어본다.
그리고 로보트 음성의 한 문장이 끝날 때까지 듣는다.

주변인은 주로 전철이나
시외버스를 타고 다닌다.
때로는 목숨 내놓고
총알 택시를 타기도 한다.
행복의 이데올로기를 믿는
행복한 사람들을 부러워하며,
서울의 탱탱한 표면장력을 그리워하며,
그 속으로 이입되기를
무수히 갈망하고 무수히 증오하면서,
표면에서 표면으로
주변에서 주변으로
가장자리에서 가장자리로
주변인은 정처없이 지도를 어지럽히며
하염없이 시간을 혼선시키며 굴러다닌다.

기억의 집

⬝◻◼ ‖ ◼◻⬝

PORTRAIT OF A SUBURBANITE

Though each time he learns the grammar of this world,
each time he forgets.
Whether the world is anesthetized
or his skull is anesthetized,
each time he cannot decide.
From matter to spirituality, from spirit to materiality,
their paths of migration he knows so well,
yet sometimes he knows nothing at all.

A suburbanite habitually restlessly awaits
the moment of the newspaper delivery,
the moment of the television broadcast.
A suburbanite occasionally calls
116 without the area code
to see if the only clock in his house is correct.
Then listens to the robot-voice till the sentence ends.

A suburbanite usually commutes
by subway or by city bus.
At times at the risk of his life
he takes bullet-speed taxis.
Envying the happy people
who believe in the ideology of happiness,
yearning for Seoul's high surface tension
innumerably craving and innumerably loathing
to be drawn into it,
from surface to surface
from periphery to periphery
from fringe to fringe,
a suburbanite rolls around
aimlessly confusing maps, ceaselessly entangling times.

삼십대

철없어 흘리던 피는 달디달지만,
때로는 몇 개의 열매도 맺었지만,
철들어 흘리는 피는 왜 이리 쓰디쓸까.

우리는 벌써 중년
자칫하다가는 중견
하마터면 중늙은이
오 이 삶의 중노동!

기억하시는지 그대들,
그 시절 그 노래를.
(애들아 나와라
달 따러 가자
장대 들고 망태 들고
뒷동산으로)
혹은
(강물아 흘러흘러
어디로 가니
넓은 세상 보고 싶어
바다로 간다)

⬚■⬚ ‖ ■⬚▫

THIRTIES

How sweet was the blood shed in immaturity,
occasionally it even bore a few fruits,
yet how come this bitter is the blood shed in maturity.

We are already middle-aged
almost old-timer
nearly elderly
oh heavy labors of this life!

I wonder if you remember
the songs of our youth.
(Come on out my friends
let's go pluck the moon
Grab a pole, grab a net
let's go up the hill in back)
or
(Flow and flow, oh river
where are you going?
Longing to see the wide world
I'm going to the sea)[19]

---

[19] These lyrics come from two Korean children's songs, "Dal-ddareo Gaja [Let's go pluck the moon]" and "Sinaenmul [The brook]."

수신인은 이미

수신인은 이미 죽었는데,
누가 암호를 보내는가.
이 물 속 같은 고요를 뚫고서……

어느 집에선가
어느 허공에선가
아니 어느 먼 먼 나라에선가

한세상 아득히 떨어져
고즈넉이 1세기를 울리고 있는
응답받지 못할 전화벨 소리.

창가에서
창가의 無爲의 침상에서
나는 한평생을 손짓으로
흘려, 흘려보낸다.

기억의 집

□·■ ‖ ■·□

RECEIVER IS ALREADY

The receiver is already dead,
yet who is sending the code?
Piercing through this underwater silence ...

In some house
in some empty space
or in some faraway country

from a lifetime's distance
ringing placidly for a century,
the phone that cannot be answered.

By the window
by the window on the bed of ennui
I dribble, dribble away
my lifetime with hand signals.

파괴의 집

사방팔방으로 바람, 바람 소리.
바람 파도에 포위된 집,
누울 곳 없는 삼십칠 세.

없는 꿈과 있는 현실,
그 사이에서 바람—
바람 소리가 날 흔들어댄다.

영원히 뿌리 없는
허공의 房, 허방의 집.

허망하고 허망하여
이 집을 파괴합니다.
이 집을 복원하지 마십시오.
행여, 이 위에 기념 건물을 세우지 마십시오.
명실공히, 이 집은 파괴의 집입니다.

HOUSE OF DESTRUCTION

Wind, sounds of wind from all directions.
The house besieged by waves of wind,
a thirty-seven year old with nowhere to rest.

Nonexistent dreams and existent realities,
from in-between, wind—
sounds of wind rattle me.

The forever rootless
room in the empty air, house in a hollow.

Groundless groundless
I destroy this house.
Do not restore this house.
By no means, build no memorial on this site.
In reality as well as in name, this is the house
    of destruction.

기도하지 않으리라

촛불이 타고 있는 동안은
이 환한 불빛에 기대리라.
심장이 타고 있는 동안은
이 따스한 온기에 기대리라.

촛불이 타고 있는 동안은
심장이 타고 있는 동안은
결코 결코 기도하지 않으리라.

나 죽은 뒤, 나도 모르는
나의 기원만이 이승 저승
홀로 헤맨다 할지라도

내 심장 한 개의 촛불로 만들어
온밤내 태우기만 하리라.
결코 결코 기도하지 않으리라.

기억의 집

⬛ ‖ ⬛

NEVER EVER WILL I PRAY

While the candle is burning
I will rely on this glowing light.
While my heart is burning
I will rely on this genial warmth.

While the candle is burning
while my heart is burning
never ever will I pray.

After my death, even if my prayer
which is unknown even to myself
wanders alone in this world and the next,

make my heart into a candle,
I'll only burn that all night long.
Never ever will I pray.

前夜

밤이면 보편적 어둠에 의해
아니 차라리 배타적 불빛들에 의해
외부와 내부, 상부와 하부
중심부와 주변부가
호화롭게 공존한다.
그러나 내 방의 내부만은
내 방의 내부 속에 닫혀 있다.

저 지겨운 짐보따리 책보따리
추억의 보따리, 절망의 보따리, 희망의 보따리
갈테면 가라지 하는 푸르른 청춘과
가지 말라 가지 말라 하는 누르른 청춘의
끝도 없고 피도 없는 건조한 싸움.

하나의 정거장일 뿐,
지상의 영원한 집은 없다.
이미 깨어진 너의 집은 없다.

그러니 가라, 가서 자라.
교과서에서 배웠듯,
"낮은 베개 높이 베고."

(경험이 네 어머니이며
未知가 네 아버지인 것을)

⬚⬚⬛ ‖ ⬛⬚⬚

THE NIGHT BEFORE

At night by the common darkness,
no, rather by exclusive lights,
exterior and interior, upper and lower,
central and peripheral parts
luxuriously coexist.
Yet my room's interior alone
is enclosed in my room's interior.

Those wearisome bundles
of luggage, books, memories, despairs, hopes
and arid, endless, bloodless fights
between the greenish youths who goad go-if-you-want
and the yellowish youths who plead don't-go-don't-go.

Merely a station,
there is no permanent house on earth.
Already broken, your house is nowhere.

Therefore off you go, go and sleep.
As you learned from textbooks,
"Rest your head high on a low pillow."

(For experience is your mother
and the unknown your father.)

고통의 춤

바람이 독점한 세상.
저 드센 바람 함대,
등 푸른 식인 상어떼.

반사적으로 부풀어오르는 내 방광.
오늘밤의 싸움은 팽팽하다.
나는 그것을 예감한다.

그리하여 이제 휘황한
고통의 춤은 시작되고,
슬픔이여 보라,
네 리듬에 맞추어
내가 춤을 추느니
이 유연한 팔과 다리,
평생토록 내 몸이
얼마나 잘
네 리듬에 길들여졌느냐.

DANCE OF PAIN

The world monopolized by wind.
Those mighty fleets of wind,
gangs of man-eating blueback sharks.

Reflexively swelling bladder of mine.
Tonight's fight is tight.
I have a hunch.

Hence the brilliant
dance of pain starts now—
as I dance to your rhythm
oh Sadness, look,
for all my life
how well this body,
these flexible arms and legs,
have been tamed
by your rhythm.

□□□ **III** □□□

未忘 혹은 備忘

UNREADY TO FORGET
OR
READY TO REMEMBER

未忘 혹은 備忘 1

아무도 모르리라.
그 세월이 어떻게 흘러갔는지.
아무도 말하지 않으리라.
그 세월의 내막을.

세월은 내게 뭉텅뭉텅
똥덩이나 던져주면서
똥이나 먹고 살라면서
세월은 마구잡이로 그냥,
내 앞에서 내 뒤에서
내 정신과 육체의 한가운데서,
저 불변의 세월은
흘러가지도 못하는 저 세월은
내게 똥이나 먹이면서
나를 무자비하게 그냥 살려두면서.

██ ▌▌▌ ██

UNREADY TO FORGET OR
READY TO REMEMBER 1

No one will know
how that time flew by.
No one will tell
its inside story.

Lump after lump
time flung shit at me
bidding me live on shit:
time just randomly,
from before me from behind me
from the middle of my body and spirit;
that immutable time
that immobile time
force-fed me shit alone,
viciously keeping me just alive.

未忘 혹은 備忘 2

먹지 않으려고
뱉지 않으려고
언제나 앙다물린 오관들.
그러나 언제나 삼켜지고
뱉아져나오는
이 조건반사적 자동반복적
삶의 쓰레기들.

목숨은 처음부터 오물이었다.

未忘 혹은 備忘

□□□ ||| □□□

UNREADY TO FORGET OR
READY TO REMEMBER 2

Try not to eat
try not to puke
always shut tight the five sensory organs.
Yet constantly gorged
and disgorged, these
conditioned-reflexive autonomic-recursive
wastes of life.

Life was filth from the beginning.

未忘 혹은 備忘 3

생명의 욕된 가지 끝에서
울고 있는 죽음의 새,
죽음의 헛된 가지 끝에서
울고 있는 삶의 새.

한 마리 새의 향방에 관하여
아무도 의심하지 않으리라
하늘은 늘 푸르를 것이다.
보이지 않게 비약의 길들과
추락의 길들을 예비한 채.

마침내의 착륙이 아니라
마침내의 추락을 예감하며
날아오르는 새의 비상—
파문과 파문 사이에서 춤추는
작은 새의 상한 깃털.

UNREADY TO FORGET OR
READY TO REMEMBER 3

Cawing on its shameful branch-tip
of life, a bird of death.
Cawing on its futile branch-tip
of death, a bird of life.

No one will doubt
the bearings of a single bird.
The sky will always be blue
ready with invisible paths
for flight and fall.

Divining not the last perch
but the final plummet,
a soaring bird's flight—
dancing between the ripples,
a tiny bird's broken feather.

未忘 혹은 備忘 4

넘치는 현존의 거리,
그만큼 또한 넘치는 부재적 실존들이여.
그 모든 부재들 중의 부재로서
나 피어났네.
검은 독버섯처럼.

뛰기 싫어 내 인생은 지각했고
걷기 싫어 내 인생은 불참했지.

오 그 모든 빛나는—
내가 불참했던,
오 그 모든 빛나는—
내가 부재했던,
그 자리들이여.
이제 내가 내 부재의 그림자로서
전 세계 위에 뻗어 누우려 하네.

UNREADY TO FORGET OR
READY TO REMEMBER 4

Streets overflowing with present existences,
overflowing as well, oh absent existences.
As one absence among all those absences
I sprouted.
Like a black poison-toadstool.

Since I detested running, my life was late.
Since I detested walking, my life was missing.

Oh all those shining—
I was missing.
Oh all those shining—
I was absent.
Oh the posts.
Now as a shadow of my own absence
I'm about to sprawl over this entire world.

未忘 혹은 備忘 5

어떻게 잠 속으로 걸어들어가야 할 것인지.
이제 개들은 머뭇거리며 골목 안으로 꼬리를 숨기고
침묵은 오래도록 홀로 신음할 것이다.

잠으로 들어가는 저 입구가 두렵다.
검은 굴 속에서 꿈은 또 물고 늘어질 것이다.
꿈은 물어뜯고 물어뜯을 것이다.
그리고 그때마다 악몽의 환각이,
두려운 생시의 파편들이 번갯불처럼 번쩍일 것이다.
한 테마의 연속적인 꿈들과
그 사이의 단절된 악몽의 환각들의 폭발.
잠으로 들어가는 저 입구가 두렵다.

그리고 내일 아침이면, 독한 하이타이로
수백번 빨아 헹구고 쥐어짠
거덜난 누더기 옷감처럼 나는 또다시
아침의 햇빛 속에 내동댕이쳐져 있을 것이다.

⊡ ◻ ◼   ‖   ◼ ◻ ⊡

UNREADY TO FORGET OR
READY TO REMEMBER 5

How to walk into sleep.
Now dogs will hesitantly hide their tails in the alley
and the silence will moan alone for a long time.

I dread that entry into sleep.
Again in that black tunnel dreams will bite and pull.
Dreams will rend and rend.
And each time the nightmarish hallucinations,
those dreadful shrapnels of reality will flash like
    lightning.
Explosions of successive dreams on one theme
and of broken nightmarish hallucinations in between.
I dread that entry into sleep.

And by tomorrow morning,
like a rag tattered by countless harsh
washings, rinsings and wringings,
I will be thrown out again in the morning sunlight.

未忘 혹은 備忘 6

말로든 살로든 못내 부비고
싶어하는 한 마리의 포유동물.
그 뇌 속 회백질의 긴 회랑 속에서
언제나 울리고 있는 발자욱 소리들.
사라지지 않는 발자욱 소리들.

그래, 이 시간에도 추억들이,
차디찬 도랑물 속에 추억들이,
눈 꼭꼭 감은 시체들이 줄지어 떠내려가고,
기억의 짐을 싣고 밤배는 또 고단히
요단강을 거슬러오를 것이다.

□□■ ‖ ■□□

UNREADY TO FORGET OR
READY TO REMEMBER 6

One mammal ever craving to be caressed
whether with words or with flesh.
In the long gray-matter gallery of its brain
ever-ringing footsteps,
never-fading footsteps.

Yes, even at this moment, recollections,
in chilly ditch water, recollections, those
corpses with tightly shut eyes must drift down in a row
and a night ship loaded with memories
must sail again wearily up the Jordan River.

未忘 혹은 備忘 7

밤이 온다.
모든 길들이 뿔뿔이 흩어진다.
누군가 한 생애의 눈시울을 감고
어디선가 검은 커튼이 내려진다.

오 늦게, 너무나 늦게서야 왔구나.
후회처럼 빠르게 내리는 서리.
회한처럼 빠르게 쌓이는 눈.

자욱히 내리는 시간의 미립자 속에서
두 발은 처음부터 존재하지 않았던 듯하고
온힘으로 내리쳐도
이 밤의 안개는 끌 수가 없다.

(내가 죽었다 깨어나도
이 밤은 아직 이 밤일 것이다)

∙□■ ‖ ■∙□

UNREADY TO FORGET OR
READY TO REMEMBER 7

Night comes.
Roads disperse in all directions.
Someone closes his eyes over a lifetime,
somewhere black curtains are lowered.

Oh late, too late it came.
Frost forming as fast as regrets.
Snow heaping as fast as remorse.

In these densely falling particles of time
it is as if these two feet never existed
and though I strike out with utmost force,
tonight's fog is impossible to dissipate.

(Even if I resurrect after my death
this night will still be this night.)

未忘 혹은 備忘 8

내 무덤, 푸르고
푸르러져
푸르름 속에 함몰되어
아득히 그 흔적조차 없어졌을 때,
그때 비로소
개울들 늘 이쁜 물소리로 가득하고
길들 모두 명상의 침묵으로 가득하리니
그때 비로소
삶 속의 죽음의 길 혹은 죽음 속의 삶의 길
새로 하나 트이지 않겠는가

□□■ ||| ■□□

UNREADY TO FORGET OR
READY TO REMEMBER 8

My tomb, green,
turns ever so green,
collapses into the greenness,
vanishes without a trace,
then finally
brooks will brim eternally with the sweet hum of water,
paths will brim entirely with the serene hush
    of meditation,
then finally
won't it freshly open
a path to death in life or a path to life in death.

未忘 혹은 備忘 9

집이 산절로 산이요
집이 수절로 물이요
그러나 집이 들끓는 불이요

집이 넘치는 술이요
집이 끝끝내 채워지지 않는 빈 잔이요.
집이 처처에 바람이요
집의 몸통에 자율신경 장애가 생겼소.

집이 큰 파도 속의 일엽편주요
집이 인적 없는 사막이요
집이 가도 가도 끝없는 원시림이요
집이 온통 절간이요
집이 도대체가 길이요

집이 길 아닌 온갖 길 위에 둥둥 떠 있소.

□□■ ‖ ■□□

UNREADY TO FORGET OR
READY TO REMEMBER 9

The house is a mountain alive
the house is water chaste
but the house is fire seething

The house is alcohol overflowing
the house is an empty cup terminally unfillable.
The house has wind in every quarter
the house has an autonomic neuropathy in its torso.

The house is a tiny skiff on massive waves
the house is a desert uninhabited
the house is a forest virgin and infinite
the house is a temple entire
yet the house is a path somehow

The house floats buoyantly above all the pathless passes.

未忘 혹은 備忘 10

비애여 네 얼굴을 보고 싶다
네 이목구비를 보고 싶다

(이 시대 비애의 얼굴은 무슨 부분들로 이루어진 것인지
한 사람이 한 시대가 걸어가는 그 행로 속에
이 무슨 비애의 돌덩어리들이 이리도 서걱이는지)

비애여 오늘밤 꿈 속에서 단 한번이라도
네 진정한 이목구비를 보고 싶다,

그리고 마지막으로 확고하게 결정하고 싶다,
네 얼굴에 키스를 해줄 것인가
아니면
네 얼굴에 똥칠을 해줄 것인가를

UNREADY TO FORGET OR
READY TO REMEMBER 10

Sorrow, I want to see your face.
I want to see your features.

(What constitutes the face of sorrow in this age?
And on the path of a person, or an age
what are all these noisy stones of sorrow?)

Sorrow, tonight in my dream, even if only once
I want to see your true features,

and I want to decide definitely at last,
whether to kiss your face
or
to smear shit on it.

未忘 혹은 備忘 11

혹시나 필요로 한다면
한 인간의 죽은 형적 산 형적을 필요로 한다면
다 남김없이 주고 다 남김없이 벗어주리라
내 치욕의 망토로 혹 그대들이 따스함을 얻을 수 있다면
그대들이 즐겨 타인의 치욕에서 자신의 영광을 찾을
수 있는 사람들이라면

(그러나 다만, 그 모든 결국까지도 넘어서
나는 항시 중도에 있었으므로,
그 모든 결국이 나에겐 항시 도중이었으므로,
오 그 모든 미래가 나의 현재였으므로.)

未忘 혹은 備忘

□□■ ‖ ■□□

UNREADY TO FORGET OR
READY TO REMEMBER 11

If you ever need them,
if you need someone's vestiges, dead or alive
I will give all away, strip all away.
If you can ever warm yourselves with my
        mantle of shame,
if you are those who can enjoy finding their own
        glory in other's shame.

(Only because, even beyond all those finalities
I was always in the middle of the road,
because all those finalities were to me always passages,
oh because all those futures were my presents.)

未忘 혹은 備忘 12

또 깜깜한 하루
귀멀고 눈멀은

내 삶의 생존 증명서는
이 먼지들의 끝없는 필적
내가 잠든 동안에도 먼지들은
내 벌려진 원고 혹은 노트 위에 알 수 없는 상형문자들을 써놓고

이 생존의 먼지 이 생존의 오물들은 사라지지 않고
마침내 내 화려한 종말을 장식할 것이다

그러나 그 먼지에 뒤덮인 원고지 속의 혹은 노트 속의
먼 길을 걸어 나는 기필코 그대들에게,
비로소 최후로 닿고 싶다

늘 언제나 절박한 현재 시각 현재 상황인
밤의 멜로디,
혹은 밥의 멜로디 속에서

□□■ ||| ■□□

UNREADY TO FORGET OR
READY TO REMEMBER 12

Another dark day
deaf and blind

life's certificate of my survival
is this dust's endless script.
Even as I sleep this dust will write
baffling pictographs on my open drafts or notes;

this dust of survival, this grime of survival will
not vanish but finally adorn my splendid finale.

Yet walking on that long path
through those dust-covered drafts or notes,
I want to reach you one last time at last

in present moments or situations ever-pressing,
in the melody of nights
or the melody of meals.

未忘 혹은 備忘 13

고독이 창처럼 나를 찌르러 올 때
나는 무슨 방패를 집어들어야 하나
오 내 방패는 어디 있나.
그냥 온몸 온정신이 방패인 것을.

어느 날 마침내 죽음을 동반한 고독이 찾아올 때까지는,
영원 불멸, 신생 부활의 방패인 것을.

그러므로 오늘도 고독의 창 앞에 쏟아부을
충분한 피를 준비해두자.
살아 있는 한 내 피는 항상 충분하므로

UNREADY TO FORGET OR
READY TO REMEMBER 13

When solitude comes to pierce me like a spear
what shield should I pick up,
oh where is my shield
when this bare body bare spirit alone is the shield.

Till finally one day solitude visits me with death,
the never-dying, ever-reviving shield.

Therefore once again today let me brew ample blood
to pour before the spear of solitude,
for as long as I live my blood will always be teeming.

未忘 혹은 備忘 14

나를 빨아들이는 길
나를 뱉아내는 길
빠져나올 수 없는 길
들어갈 수 없는 길

영원토록 길이 나를 가둔다
영원토록 길이 나를 해방시킨다

떠나야 할 시각이 길게 드리워진다
그가 끝나도 길은 끝나지 않을 것이다
그 길 모퉁이에 이따금씩
추억의 나무 한 그루 서 있을 것이다

우연의 형식들로 다가오는 모든 필연을 견디면서
이미 추억이 다 된 나무 한 그루
백발의 나무 한 그루 서 있을 것이다.

UNREADY TO FORGET OR
READY TO REMEMBER 14

The road that sucks me in
the road that spits me out
the road that's impossible to exit
the road that's impossible to enter

The road forever confines me.
The road forever liberates me.

The departure time ever prolongs.
The road will never end even after he is finished.
Now and then at the corner of that road
a tree of recollection will appear.

Suffering all necessities approaching in the guises of
    chance,
a tree, already almost a recollection,
a white-haired tree will appear.

未忘 혹은 備忘 15

이미 지나왔던 이 길,
이제 비로소 선택하리라.
왔던 곳으로 되돌아가는 길.

망막의 뒤편에 쌓인 응집된
추억들은 다시 한 올씩 풀려지고
기억 속의 들꽃들이 저 혼자 흔들리는 곳,

이제 처음으로 시작하는 길,
되돌아가는 길.

희망은 길고 질기며
절망은 넓고 깊은 것을……

UNREADY TO FORGET OR
READY TO REMEMBER 15

This road I've already tread,
I will take it now at last.
The road to return whence I came

where the knotted recollections piled behind my retina
disentangle once again strand by strand,
where the wild flowers in my memory waver alone,

the road I start now for the first time,
the road to return.

For hope is long and strong,
despair, wide and deep....

未忘 혹은 備忘 16

가을의 페이지가 넘길수록 깊어진다.
그리고 잠이, 마약 같은 마비의 잠이
온몸의 말초혈관부터 퍼져 올라온다.

곧 뇌중추가 항복하리라.
온 城이 가뭇없이
잠의 빙하 속에 가라앉으리라.

그러나 아직은 흔들리는 이 끝에서,
흔들리는 이 물살이 심히 어지럽구나.
물살을 잠재우든가,
떠도는 이 일엽편주를 잠재우라.

□·□ ||| □□·

UNREADY TO FORGET OR
READY TO REMEMBER 16

The pages of autumn deepen as they turn.
And sleep, narcotic paralyzing sleep
seeps up from every peripheral vessel.

Soon the central brain will surrender.
The whole castle will sink without a trace
under the glacier of sleep.

Yet still, at this quaking end,
how vertiginous is this quivering wave.
Either let this wave slumber
or send this drifting skiff to sleep.

東海

東海,
존재의 맨살.
끝없는 바닥의 어둠이자 끝없는 표피의 투명함,
상처의 흔적과 기쁨의 기억,
있음과 없음,
무한과 유한이
참으로 고요히 서로를 물고 있구나.

굳어진 상흔을 찢어 열면서
새로 돋는, 죽음의 살의 신비.
(여기까지가 네 生前
그리고 이미 네 死後이다.)
그러므로 상징은 여기서 끝내자.

未忘 혹은 備忘

⬚⬚◼ ‖ ◼⬚⬚

THE EAST SEA

The East Sea,
the raw flesh of existence.
The obscurity of a bottomless floor and the lucidity
    of a boundless epidermis,
traces of injuries and memories of joys,
being and non-being,
infinite and finite
are most serenely gnawing at each other.

Tearing open hardened scars,
growing anew, the mystery of death's flesh.
(Thus far is your lifetime
and is already your afterlife.)
Therefore, let us here finish symbolizing.

자본족

몇 행의 시라는 물건이
졸지에 만 원짜리 몇장으로 휘날릴 수 있는 시대에
똥이 곧 예술이 될 수 있고, 상품이 될 수 있는 이 시대에
쓰자, 그 까짓거, 까아아아아아아아아아아아아짓거.
영혼이란 동화책에 나오는 천사지.

돈 엄마가 돈 새끼를,
자본 엄마가 자본 새끼를 낳는,
(오 지상을 뒤덮는 자본 종족)이 세상에서
자본의 새끼의 새끼의 새끼의 새끼가 시일 수 있다면
(모든 시인은 부복하라)
오 나는 그 새끼를 키워 어미로 만들리라
인간이라는 고등 포유 동물을 넘어서는
(저 아리안족 같은)고등 자본 동물을 만들리라

곳곳에서 넘쳐나는 저 자본 동물들,
우리가 익히 잘 아는 인간들이
자본 科 파충류로 변해 가는 것을,
오 내 팔뚝에 뱀의 살 무늬가 새겨지는 것을 지켜 보는 이 슬픔
새들도 자본 자본 하며 울 날이 오리라.

(나에게 뽀스또 모단의 방식을 가르쳐 다오,
나는 왜 이렇게 정통적으로밖에 얘기할 수가 없는지.)

210   未忘 혹은 備忘

THE CAPITAL SPECIES

In an age when a poem, a thing with a few lines,
can suddenly flutter as bountiful dollar bills,
in this age when shit can instantly become art, can
    become a commodity,
let's write that damn thing, daaaaaaaaaaaaaaamn thing.
The soul is a fairy in a fairy tale.

In this world (Oh covering the earth, capital species)
where money-moms breed money-babes,
where capital-moms breed capital-babes,
if the babe of the babe of the babe of the babe of capital
    can be a poem,
(Prostrate yourselves all poets!)
oh I will raise that babe and turn it into a dam,
I will turn it into the higher capital-animal (akin
    to that Aryan race)
that will surpass the higher mammal, the human.

Overflowing everywhere, those capital-animals:
oh this sadness, witnessing humans whom
    we know so well
turn into reptiles of the genus capital,
witnessing a snakeskin pattern tattoo my forearm.
The day will come when even birds sing Capital Capital.

(Teach me please the postmodern style,
how come I can only speak orthodoxically like this.)

□□□ ‖ □□□

마흔

서른이 될 때는 높은 벼랑 끝에 서 있는 기분이었지
이 다음 발걸음부터는 가파른 내리막길을
끝도 없이 추락하듯 내려가는 거라고.
그러나 사십대는 너무도 드넓은 궁륭 같은 평야로구나
한없이 넓어, 가도 가도
벽도 내리받이도 보이지 않는,
그러나 곳곳에 투명한 유리벽이 있어,
재수없으면 쿵쿵 머리방아를 찧는 곳.

그래도 나는 단 한 가지 믿는 것이 있어서
이 마흔에 날마다, 믿는 도끼에 발등을 찍힌다.

□□□ ‖ □□□

未忘 혹은 備忘

⬚⬚◼ ‖ ◼⬚⬚

FORTIES

Turning thirty I felt as though standing on the edge of
    a high cliff
with the next step a steep downhill
descending endlessly like falling.
But what a vast vaulting field the forties are,
boundlessly vast, however far I go,
not a wall, not a descent is in sight,
yet clear glass walls stand here and there
where unlucky me might Bam! bang my head.

Nonetheless, I have faith in one and only thing
each day of my forties I get hacked in the back
    by my trusted ax.

▫▫▫ INDEX OF POEMS ▫▫▫

▫▫▫ I ▫▫▫
LOVE OF THIS AGE

CORNELL EAST ASIA SERIES

CORNELL
East Asia Series

eap.einaudi.cornell.edu/publications

CPSIA information can be obtained
at www.ICGtesting.com
Printed in the USA
LVHW091936151119
637499LV00007B/51/P